TEACHER'S PET PUBLICATIONS

LITPLAN TEACHER PACK
for
A Midsummer Night's Dream

based on the play by
William Shakespeare

Written by
Mary B. Collins

© 1996 Teacher's Pet Publications
All Rights Reserved

This **LitPlan** for William Shakespeare's
A Midsummer Night's Dream
has been brought to you by Teacher's Pet Publications, Inc.

Copyright Teacher's Pet Publications 1996
11504 Hammock Point
Berlin MD 21811

Only the student materials in this unit plan (such as worksheets,
study questions, and tests) may be reproduced multiple times
for use in the purchaser's classroom.

For any additional copyright questions,
contact Teacher's Pet Publications.

www.tpet.com

TABLE OF CONTENTS - *Midsummer Night's Dream*

Introduction	11
Unit Objectives	13
Reading Assignment Sheet	14
Unit Outline	15
Study Questions (Short Answer)	19
Quiz/Study Questions (Multiple Choice)	25
Pre-reading Vocabulary Worksheets	37
Lesson One (Introductory Lesson)	51
Nonfiction Assignment Sheet	53
Oral Reading Evaluation Form	57
Writing Assignment 1	59
Writing Assignment 2	65
Writing Assignment 3	71
Writing Evaluation Form	66
Vocabulary Review Activities	64
Extra Writing Assignments/Discussion ?s	68
Unit Review Activities	73
Unit Tests	77
Unit Resource Materials	109
Vocabulary Resource Materials	123

ABOUT THE AUTHOR
WILLIAM SHAKESPEARE

SHAKESPEARE, William (1564-1616). For more than 350 years, William Shakespeare has been the world's most popular playwright. On the stage, in the movies, and on television his plays are watched by vast audiences. People read his plays again and again for pleasure. Students reading his plays for the first time are delighted by what they find.

Shakespeare's continued popularity is due to many things. His plays are filled with action, his characters are believable, and his language is thrilling to hear or read. Underlying all this is Shakespeare's deep humanity. He was a profound student of people and he understood them. He had a great tolerance, sympathy, and love for all people, good or evil.

While watching a Shakespearean tragedy, the audience is moved and shaken. After the show the spectators are calm, washed clean of pity and terror. They are saddened but at peace, repeating the old saying, "There, but for the grace of God, go I."

A Shakespearean comedy is full of fun. The characters are lively; the dialogue is witty. In the end young lovers are wed; old babblers are silenced; wise men are content. The comedies are joyous and romantic.

Boyhood in Stratford

William Shakespeare was born in Stratford-upon-Avon, England, in 1564. This was the sixth year of the reign of Queen Elizabeth I. He was christened on April 26 of that year. The day of his birth is unknown. It has long been celebrated on April 23, the feast of St. George.

He was the third child and oldest son of John and Mary Arden Shakespeare. Two sisters, Joan and Margaret, died before he was born. The other children were Gilbert, a second Joan, Anne, Richard, and Edmund. Only the second Joan outlived William.

Shakespeare's father was a tanner and glovemaker. He was an alderman of Stratford for years. He also served a term as high bailiff, or mayor. Toward the end of his life John Shakespeare lost most of his money. When he died in 1601, he left William only a little real estate. Not much is known about Mary Shakespeare, except that she came from a wealthier family than her husband.

Stratford-upon-Avon is in Warwickshire, called the heart of England. In Shakespeare's day it was well farmed and heavily wooded. The town itself was prosperous and progressive.

The town was proud of its grammar school. Young Shakespeare went to it, although when or for how long is not known. He may have been a pupil there between his 7th and 13th years. His studies must have been mainly in Latin. The schooling was good. All four schoolmasters at the school during Shakespeare's boyhood were graduates of Oxford University.

Nothing definite is known about his boyhood. From the content of his plays, he must have learned early about the woods and fields, about birds, insects, and small animals, about trades and outdoor sports, and about the country people he later portrayed with such good humor. Then and later he picked up an amazing stock of facts about hunting, hawking, fishing, dances, music, and other arts and sports. Among other subjects, he also learned about alchemy, astrology, folklore, medicine, and law. As good writers do, he collected information both from books and
from daily observation of the world around him.

Marriage and Life in London
In 1582, when he was 18, he married Anne Hathaway. She was from Shottery, a village a mile from Stratford. Anne was seven or eight years older than Shakespeare. From this difference in their ages, a story arose that they were unhappy together. Their first daughter, Susanna, was
born in 1583. In 1585 a twin boy and girl, Hamnet and Judith, were born.

What Shakespeare did between 1583 and 1592 is not known. Various stories are told. He may have taught school, worked in a lawyer's office, served on a rich man's estate, or traveled with a company of actors. One famous story says that about 1584 he and some friends were caught poaching on the estate of Sir Thomas Lucy of Carlecote, near Warwick, and were forced to leave town. A less likely story is that he was in London in 1588. There he was supposed to have held horses for theater patrons and later to have worked in the theaters as a callboy.

By 1592, however, Shakespeare was definitely in London and was already recognized as an actor and playwright. He was then 28 years old. In that year he was referred to in another man's book for the first time. Robert Greene, a playwright, accused him of borrowing from the plays of
others.

Between 1592 and 1594, plague kept the London theaters closed most of the time. During these years Shakespeare wrote his earliest sonnets and two long narrative poems, 'Venus and Adonis' and 'The Rape of Lucrece'. Both were printed by Richard Field, a boyhood friend from Stratford. They were well received and helped establish him as a poet.

Shakespeare Prospers
Until 1598 Shakespeare's theater work was confined to a district northeast of London. This was outside the walls, in the parish of Shoreditch. Located there were two playhouses, the Theatre and the Curtain. Both were managed by James Burbage, whose son Richard Burbage was Shakespeare's friend and the greatest tragic actor of his day.

Up to 1596 Shakespeare lived near these theaters in Bishopsgate, where the North Road entered the city. Sometime between 1596 and 1599, he moved across the Thames River to a district called Bankside. There, two theaters, the Rose and the Swan, had been built by Philip
Henslowe. He was James Burbage's chief competitor in London as a theater manager.

The Burbages also moved to this district in 1598 and built the famous Globe Theatre. Its sign showed Atlas supporting the world-hence the theater's name. Shakespeare was associated with the Globe Theatre for the rest of his active life. He owned shares in it, which brought him much money.

Meanwhile, in 1597, Shakespeare had bought New Place, the largest house in Stratford. During the next three years he bought other property in Stratford and in London. The year before, his father, probably at Shakespeare's suggestion, applied for and was granted a coat of arms. It
bore the motto Non sanz droict-Not without right. From this time on, Shakespeare could write "Gentleman" after his name. This meant much to him, for in his day actors were classed legally with criminals and vagrants.

Shakespeare's name first appeared on the title pages of his printed plays in 1598. In the same year Francis Meres, in 'Palladis Tamia: Wit's Treasury', praised him as a poet and dramatist. Meres's comments on 12 of Shakespeare's plays showed that Shakespeare's genius was recognized in his own time.

Honored As Actor and Playwright
Queen Elizabeth I died in 1603. King James I followed her to the throne. Shakespeare's theatrical company was taken under the king's patronage and called the King's Company. Shakespeare and the other actors were made officers of the royal household. The theatrical company was the most successful of its time. Before it was the King's Company, it had been known as the Earl of Derby's and the Lord Chamberlain's. In 1608 the company acquired the Blackfriars Theatre. This was a smaller and more aristocratic theater than the Globe. Thereafter the company alternated between the two playhouses.

Plays by Shakespeare were performed at both theaters, at the royal court, and in the castles of the nobles. After 1603 Shakespeare probably acted little, although he was still a good actor. His favorite roles seem to have been old Adam in 'As You Like It' and the Ghost in 'Hamlet'.

In 1607, when he was 43, he may have suffered a serious physical breakdown. In the same year his older daughter Susanna married John Hall, a doctor. The next year Shakespeare's first grandchild, Elizabeth, was born. Also in 1607 his brother Edmund, who had been an actor
in London, died at the age of 27.

The Mermaid Tavern Group

About this time Shakespeare became one of the group of now-famous writers who gathered at the Mermaid Tavern in Cheapside. The club was formed by Sir Walter Raleigh. Ben Jonson was its leading spirit (see Jonson). Shakespeare was a popular member. He was admired for his talent and loved for his kindliness. Thomas Fuller, writing about 50 years later, gave an amusing account of the conversational duels between Shakespeare and Jonson:

"Many were the wit-combats betwixt him and Ben Jonson; which two I behold like a Spanish great galleon and an English man-of-war; Master Jonson (like the former) was built far higher in learning; solid, but slow, in his performances. Shakespeare, with the English man-of-war, lesser in bulk, but lighter in sailing, could turn with all tides, tack about, and take advantage of all winds, by the quickness of his wit and invention."

Jonson sometimes criticized Shakespeare harshly. Nevertheless he later wrote a eulogy of Shakespeare that is remarkable for its feeling and acuteness. In it he said:

> Leave thee alone, for the comparison
> Of all that insolent Greece or haughty Rome
> Sent forth, or since did from their ashes come.
> Triumph, my Britain, thou hast one to show
> To whom all scenes of Europe homage owe.
> He was not of an age, but for all time!
> . . . .
> Sweet Swan of Avon! what a sight it were
> To see thee in our waters yet appear,
> And make those flights upon the banks of Thames,
> That so did take Eliza, and our James!

Death and Burial at Stratford

Shakespeare retired from his theater work in 1610 and returned to Stratford. His friends from London visited him. In 1613 the Globe Theatre burned. He lost much money in it, but he was still wealthy. He shared in the building of the new Globe. A few months before the fire he bought as an investment a house in the fashionable Blackfriars district of London.

On April 23, 1616, Shakespeare died at the age of 52. This date is according to the Old Style, or Julian, calendar of his time. The New Style, or Gregorian, calendar date is May 3, 1616. He was buried in the chancel of the Church of the Holy Trinity in Stratford.

A stone slab-a reproduction of the original one, which it replaced in 1830-marks his grave. It bears an inscription, perhaps written by himself.

On the north wall of the chancel is his monument. It consists of a portrait bust enclosed in a stone frame. Below it is an inscription in Latin and English. This bust and the engraving by Martin Droeshout, prefixed to the First Folio edition of his plays (1623), are the only pictures of Shakespeare which can be accepted as showing his true likeness.

John Aubrey, an English antiquarian, wrote about Shakespeare 65 years after the poet's death. He evidently used information furnished by the son of one of Shakespeare's fellow actors. Aubrey described him as "a handsome, well-shaped man, very good company, and of a ready and pleasant smooth wit."

Shakespeare's will, still in existence, bequeathed most of his property to Susanna and her daughter. He left small mementoes to friends. He mentioned his wife only once, leaving her his "second best bed" with its furnishings.

Much has been written about this odd bequest. There is little reason to think it was a slight. Indeed, it may have been a special mark of affection. The "second best bed" was probably the one they used. The best bed was reserved for guests. At any rate, his wife was entitled by law to one third of her husband's goods and real estate and to the use of their home for life. She died in 1623.

The will contains three signatures of Shakespeare. These, with three others, are the only known specimens of his handwriting in existence. Several experts also regard some lines in the manuscript of 'Sir Thomas More' as Shakespeare's own handwriting. He spelled his name in
various ways. His father's papers show about 16 spellings. Shakspere, Shaxpere, and Shakespeare are the most common.

Did Shakespeare Really Write the Plays?
The outward events of Shakespeare's life are ordinary. He was hard-working, sober, and middle-class in his ways. He steadily gathered wealth and took good care of his family. Many people have found it impossible to believe that such a man could have written the plays. They feel that he could not have known such heights and depths of passion. They believe that the people around Shakespeare expressed little realization of his greatness. Some say that a man of his little schooling could not have learned about the professions, the aristocratic sports of hawking and hunting, the speech and manners of the upper classes.

Since the 1800's there has been a steady effort to prove that Shakespeare did not write the plays or that others did. For a long time the leading candidate was Sir Francis Bacon. Books on the Shakespeare-Bacon argument would fill a library (see Bacon, Francis). After Bacon became less
popular, the Earl of Oxford and then other men were suggested as the authors. Nearly every famous Elizabethan was named. The most recent has been Christopher Marlowe. Some people even claim that "Shakespeare" is an assumed name for a whole group of poets and playwrights.

However, some men around Shakespeare-for example, Meres in 1598 and Jonson in 1623-did recognize his worth as a man and as a writer. To argue that an obscure Stratford boy could not have become the Shakespeare of literature is to ignore the mystery of genius. His knowledge
is of the kind that could not be learned in school. It is the kind that only a genius could learn, by applying a keen intelligence to everyday life. Some great writers have had even less schooling than Shakespeare.

Few scholars take seriously these attempts to deprive Shakespeare of credit. Shakespeare's style is individual and cannot be imitated. Any good student recognizes it. It can be found nowhere else. Bacon is a poor candidate for the honor. Great as he was, he was certainly not a poet.

How the Plays Came Down to Us
Since the 1700's scholars have worked over the text of Shakespeare's plays. They have had to do so because the plays were badly printed, and no original manuscripts of them survive.

In Shakespeare's day plays were not usually printed under the author's supervision. When a playwright sold a play to his company, he lost all rights to it. He could not sell it again to a publisher without the company's consent. When the play was no longer in demand on the
stage, the company itself might sell the manuscript. Plays were eagerly read by the Elizabethan public. This was even more true during the plague years, when the theaters were closed. It was also true during times of business depression. Sometimes plays were taken down in
shorthand and sold. At other times, a dismissed actor would write down the play from memory and sell it.

About half of Shakespeare's plays were printed during his lifetime in small, cheap pamphlets called quartos. Most of these were made from fairly accurate manuscripts. A few were in garbled form.

In 1623, seven years after Shakespeare's death, his collected plays were published in a large, expensive volume called the First Folio. It contains all his plays except two of which he wrote only part-'Pericles' and 'Two Noble Kinsmen'. It also has the first engraved portrait of
Shakespeare.

This edition was authorized by Shakespeare's acting group, the King's Company. Some of the plays in it were printed from the accurate quartos and some from manuscripts in the theater. It is certain that many of these manuscripts were in Shakespeare's own handwriting. Others were copies. Still others, like the 'Midsummer Night's Dream' manuscript, had been revised by another dramatist.

Shakespearean scholars have been determining what Shakespeare actually wrote. They have done so by studying the language, stagecraft, handwriting, and printing of the period and by carefully examining and comparing the different editions. They have modernized spelling and punctuation, supplied stage directions, explained difficult passages, and made the plays easier for the modern reader to understand.

Another hard task has been to find out when the plays were written. About half of them have no definite date of composition. The plays themselves have been searched for clues. Other books have been examined. Scholars have tried to match events in Shakespeare's life with the subject matter of his plays.

These scholars have used detective methods. They have worked with clues, deduction, shrewd reasoning, and external and internal evidence. External evidence consists of actual references in other books. Internal evidence is made up of verse tests and a study of the poet's imagery and figures of speech, which changed from year to year.

The verse tests follow the idea that a poet becomes more skillful with practice. Scholars long ago noticed that in his early plays Shakespeare used little prose, much rhyme, and certain types of rhythmical and metrical regularity. As he grew older he used more prose, less rhyme,
and greater freedom and variety in rhythm and meter. From these facts, scholars have figured out the dates of those plays that had none.

Shakespeare As a Dramatist
The facts about Shakespeare are interesting in themselves, but they have little to do with his place in literature. Shakespeare wrote his plays to give pleasure. It is possible to spoil that pleasure by giving too much attention to his life, his times, and the problem of figuring out what he actually wrote. He can be enjoyed in book form, in the theater, or on television without our knowing any of these things.

Some difficulties stand in the way of this enjoyment. Shakespeare wrote more than 350 years ago. The language he used is naturally somewhat different from the language of today. Besides, he wrote in verse. Verse permits a free use of words that may not be understood by some readers. His plays are often fanciful. This may not appeal to matter-of-fact people who are used to modern realism. For all these reasons, readers may find him difficult. The worst handicap to enjoyment is the notion that Shakespeare is a "classic," a writer to be approached with awe.

The way to escape this last difficulty is to remember that Shakespeare wrote his plays for everyday people and that many in the audience were uneducated. They looked upon him as a funny, exciting, and lovable entertainer, not as a great poet. People today should read him as the people in his day listened to him. The excitement and enjoyment of the plays will banish most of the difficulties.

--- Courtesy of Compton's Learning Company

INTRODUCTION - *Midsummer Night's Dream*

This unit has been designed to develop students' reading, writing, thinking, and language skills through exercises and activities related to *Midsummer Night's Dream* by William Shakespeare. It includes twenty-four lessons, supported by extra resource materials.

The **introductory lesson** introduces students to Shakespeare and his times through a group research project. Following the introductory activity, students are given a transition to explain how the activity relates to the play they are about to read. Following the transition, students are given the materials they will be using during the unit. At the end of the lesson, students begin the pre-reading work for the first reading assignment.

The **reading assignments** are approximately thirty pages each; some are a little shorter while others are a little longer. Students have approximately 15 minutes of pre-reading work to do prior to each reading assignment. This pre-reading work involves reviewing the study questions for the assignment and doing some vocabulary work for some challenging vocabulary words they will encounter in their reading.

The **study guide questions** are fact-based questions; students can find the answers to these questions right in the text. These questions come in two formats: short answer or multiple choice. The best use of these materials is probably to use the short answer version of the questions as study guides for students (since answers will be more complete), and to use the multiple choice version for occasional quizzes. It might be a good idea to make transparencies of your answer keys for the overhead projector.

The **vocabulary work** is intended to enrich students' vocabularies as well as to aid in the students' understanding of the play. Prior to each reading assignment, students will complete a two-part worksheet for approximately 10 vocabulary words in the upcoming reading assignment. Part I focuses on students' use of general knowledge and contextual clues by giving the sentence in which the word appears in the text. Students are then to write down what they think the words mean based on the words' usage. Part II nails down the definitions of the words by giving students dictionary definitions of the words and having students match the words to the correct definitions based on the words' contextual usage. Students should then have an understanding of the words when they meet them in the text.

After each reading assignment, students will go back and formulate answers for the study guide questions. Discussion of these questions serves as a **review** of the most important events and ideas presented in the reading assignments.

After students complete reading the work, there is a **vocabulary review** lesson which pulls together all of the fragmented vocabulary lists for the reading assignments and gives students a review of all of the words they have studied.

Following the vocabulary review, a lesson is devoted to the **extra discussion questions/writing assignments**. These questions focus on interpretation, critical analysis and personal response, employing a variety of thinking skills and adding to the students' understanding of the play.

The **project** which follows the discussion questions has students working together to create a variety show full of different kinds of humor. Each student is assigned a kind of humor his "act" must portray.

There are three **writing assignments** in this unit, each with the purpose of informing, persuading, or having students express personal opinions. The first assignment is to inform: students take the information they have gathered through research, group work and class discussion and organize it into a composition. The second assignment is to persuade: students create a humorous puppet sketch to use to persuade a little boy or girl not to be afraid in the dark. The third assignment is to give students the opportunity to be creative and express their own opinions: students choose one of several topics related to the themes or ideas in the play.

In addition, there is a **nonfiction reading assignment**. Students are required to read a piece of nonfiction related in some way to *Midsummer Night's Dream*. After reading their nonfiction pieces, students will fill out a worksheet on which they answer questions regarding facts, interpretation, criticism, and personal opinions. During one class period, students make **oral presentations** about the nonfiction pieces they have read. This not only exposes all students to a wealth of information, it also gives students the opportunity to practice **public speaking**. This nonfiction assignment is done in conjunction with the introductory research assignment.

The **review lesson** pulls together all of the aspects of the unit. The teacher is given four or five choices of activities or games to use which all serve the same basic function of reviewing all of the information presented in the unit.

The **unit test** comes in two formats: all multiple choice-matching-true/false or with a mixture of matching, short answer, multiple choice, and composition. As a convenience, two different tests for each format have been included. There is also an advanced short answer version of the unit test.

There are additional **support materials** included with this unit. The **Unit Resource** section includes suggestions for an in-class library, crossword and word search puzzles related to the play, and extra vocabulary worksheets. There is a list of **bulletin board ideas** which gives the teacher suggestions for bulletin boards to go along with this unit. In addition, there is a list of **extra class activities** the teacher could choose from to enhance the unit or as a substitution for an exercise the teacher might feel is inappropriate for his/her class. **Answer keys** are located directly after the **reproducible student materials** throughout the unit. Only the student materials may be reproduced for use in the teacher's classroom without infringement of copyrights.

UNIT OBJECTIVES - *Midsummer Night's Dream*

1. Through reading Shakespeare's *Midsummer Night's Dream* students will study different kinds of comedy/humor and the history of various kinds of humor.

2. Students will demonstrate their understanding of the text on four levels: factual, interpretive, critical and personal.

3. Students will create a variety show using different kinds of humor.

4. Students will study Shakespearian comedy.

5. Students will study the theme "love is blind" and the related themes of love causing people to be unreasonable and unpredictable.

6. Students will study the motif of dreams and dreaming in the play.

7. Students will examine Shakespeare's use of language.

8. Students will be given the opportunity to practice reading aloud and silently to improve their skills in each area.

9. Students will answer questions to demonstrate their knowledge and understanding of the main events and characters in *Midsummer Night's Dream* as they relate to the author's theme development.

10. Students will enrich their vocabularies and improve their understanding of the play through the vocabulary lessons prepared for use in conjunction with the play.

11. The writing assignments in this unit are geared to several purposes:
    a. To have students demonstrate their abilities to inform, to persuade, or to express their own personal ideas
        Note: Students will demonstrate ability to write effectively to <u>inform</u> by developing and organizing facts to convey information. Students will demonstrate the ability to write effectively to <u>persuade</u> by selecting and organizing relevant information, establishing an argumentative purpose, and by designing an appropriate strategy for an identified audience. Students will demonstrate the ability to write effectively to <u>express personal ideas</u> by selecting a form and its appropriate elements.
    b. To check the students' reading comprehension
    c. To make students think about the ideas presented by the play
    d. To encourage logical thinking
    e. To provide an opportunity to practice good grammar and improve students' use of the English language.

READING ASSIGNMENT SHEET - *Midsummer Night's Dream*

Date Assigned	Reading Assignment Act: Scene(s)	Completion Date
	I	
	II	
	III	
	IV	
	V	

UNIT OUTLINE - *Midsummer Night's Dream*

1 Library	2 Nonfiction Reports	3 Materials Parts PV Act I	4 Read Act I	5 Read Act I
6 Study ?s Act I Parts Act II PV Act II	7 Read Act II	8 Writing Assignment 1	9 Study ?s Act II Parts Act III PV Act III	10 Read Act III
11 Read Act III	12 Study ?s Act III Parts Act IV PV Act IV	13 Read Act IV	14 Study ?s Act IV Parts Act V PV Act V	15 Read Act V
16 Study ?s Act V Vocabulary	17 Writing Assignment 2	18 Project	19 Project	20 Extra Questions
21 Writing Assignment 3	22 Film	23 Review	24 Test	(Variety Show)

Key: P = Preview Study Questions   V = Vocabulary Work   R = Read

STUDY GUIDE QUESTIONS

SHORT ANSWER STUDY GUIDE QUESTIONS - *A Midsummer Night's Dream*

Act I
1. What are Theseus and Hippolyta discussing at the play's start?
2. How does Hippolyta come to be betrothed to Theseus?
3. Why is Egeus disturbed?
4. What will be Hermia's fate if she refuses to marry Demetrius?
5. To what do Lysander and Hermia agree?
6. What hope does Helena have by telling Demetrius of Lysander and Hermia's flight?
7. Who are the characters in scene two, and what do they plan?

Act II
1. Why is Oberon angry with his queen?
2. On what mission does Oberon send Puck?
3. Upon overhearing Demetrius and Helena, what does Oberon command Puck to do?
4. Upon whose eyes does Puck apply the potion?
5. When he wakes up, who does Lysander see and love?
6. What is Helena's reaction to Lysander's words of love?
7. To where has Lysander disappeared when Hermia awakes?

Act III
1. Why does Bottom want a prologue written for the play?
2. What has Puck done to Bottom?
3. Identify the speaker: "Tie up my love's tongue, bring him silently."
4. What news does Puck bring Oberon?
5. Why does Oberon send Puck to fetch Helena?
6. What is Helena's situation at this point in the play?
7. What does Helena suppose of Hermia?
8. What does Hermia think Helena has done?
9. Why does Oberon send Puck to confuse the two young men?
10. What remedy corrects the crossed-loved couples?

Act IV
1. Why does Titania give Oberon the child?
2. How does Oberon find Titania and Bottom?
3. Why does Oberon remove the spell he has cast over his queen?
4. Finding the two couples asleep in the wood and learning of their more balanced love, what order does Theseus give?
5. What news does Bottom bring his companions?

A Midsummer Night's Dream Study Questions Page 2

<u>Act V</u>
1. Why do you think Shakespeare included a play within a play?
2. What do the fairies do after the palace goes to sleep?
3. Who does Puck address at the play's end?
4. What is the purpose of this last speech?

ANSWER KEY: SHORT ANSWER STUDY GUIDE QUESTIONS
A Midsummer Night's Dream

Act I

1. What are Theseus and Hippolyta discussing at the play's start?
    They are discussing their wedding which is supposed to take place in four days' time.

2. How does Hippolyta come to be betrothed to Theseus?
    He has defeated her in battle and won her hand in marriage as a peace settlement or perhaps as the spoils of victory.

3. Why is Egeus disturbed?
    He wants his daughter, Hermia, to marry Demetrius, but she loves and desires to marry Lysander.

4. What will be Hermia's fate if she refuses to marry Demetrius?
    She may choose to die or to live as a cloistered nun.

5. To what do Lysander and Hermia agree?
    They agree to meet on the next night in a wood a league from Athens and from there to make their way to the remote home of Lysander's aunt where they can be married and safe from Athen's cruel punishment and separation.

6. What hope does Helena have by telling Demetrius of Lysander and Hermia's flight?
    She anticipates the sweet pain of following him to and from the appointed wood while he pursues Hermia.

7. Who are the characters in scene two, and what do they plan?
    They are six craftsmen of Athens who plan to perform the tragedy of Pyramus and Thisby as an entertainment to honor the duke's wedding day.

Act II

1. Why is Oberon angry with his queen?
    She keeps a young boy as her attendant, and Oberon wants the young boy for himself. She refuses to share the lovely child with him.

2. On what mission does Oberon send Puck?
    Oberon sends Puck to find a flower that has been struck by Cupid's arrow so that he may anoint the sleeping Titania, causing her to blindly love the first creature she sees upon awaking.

3. Upon overhearing Demetrius and Helena, what does Oberon command Puck to do?
> He tells Puck to find the Athenian couple and anoint the youth's eyes as he sleeps so that upon waking he will see the maid and love her.

4. Upon whose eyes does Puck apply the potion?
> He does Lysander's eyes by mistake.

5. When he wakes up, who does Lysander see and love?
> He sees Helena.

6. What is Helena's reaction to Lysander's words of love?
> She thinks he is cruelly teasing her.

7. To where has Lysander disappeared when Hermia awakes?
> He has gone to follow Helena, whom he now loves.

Act III

1. Why does Bottom want a prologue written for the play?
> He wants one written so that his character can read it to the audience, assuring them that no harm will come to the actors either by sword or by lion. He thinks the ladies will go into a swoon or else panic.

2. What has Puck done to Bottom?
> He has changed his head into that of an ass.

3. Identify the speaker: "Tie up my love's tongue, bring him silently."
> Titania was instructing her fairies to bring Bottom to her bower.

4. What news does Puck bring Oberon?
> He tells Oberon that Titania is in love with a monster, an ass; and that he has successfully dosed the Athenian's eyes.

5. Why does Oberon send Puck to fetch Helena?
> He realizes that another Athenian youth was dosed by Puck by mistake and that now a maid has lost her true love (Lysander) and the intended youth (Demetrius) is still repulsing Helena. While Puck is away, Oberon charms Demetrius to love Helena when he sees her again.

6. What is Helena's situation at this point in the play?
> She is now loved by both Lysander and Demetrius and she believes that they have conspired to play a cruel prank on her.

7. What does Helena suppose of Hermia?
   She thinks that Hermia has joined in the malicious prank with Lysander and Demetrius.

8. What does Hermia think Helena has done?
   She thinks that out of jealousy she has made known her taller height and therefore her greater value of the two maids.

9. Why does Oberon send Puck to confuse the two young men?
   They are going to fight over Helena, so Oberon has Puck make the night darken and cloudy and use his voice to lead them away from each other and to sleep.

10. What remedy corrects the crossed-loved couples?
    Puck drips the potion on Lysander's eyes so he will love his former sweetheart, Hermia. He leaves Demetrius loving Helena.

Act IV

1. Why does Titania give Oberon the child?
   She cares for him no longer now that she has Bottom on whom to dote.

2. How does Oberon find Titania and Bottom?
   They are asleep in each other's arms.

3. Why does Oberon remove the spell he has cast over his queen?
   He has the boy and now he pities his queen her silly new love-pet. He wants her back to her true self.

4. Finding the two couples asleep in the wood and learning of their more balanced love, what order does Theseus give?
   He orders that they should follow him and Hippolyta to be married with them at the temple.

5. What news does Bottom bring his companions?
   He says that their play has been chosen by the duke as an entertainment. They must now get ready and meet at the palace.

Act V

1. Why do you think Shakespeare included a play within a play?
   The story of Pyramus and Thisby is an ancient tale well known to the audiences in Shakespeare's time. The audience of *A Midsummer Night's Dream* could join in with the jests and comments.

2. What do the fairies do after the palace goes to sleep?
    Oberon sends them off throughout the house to sing and dance and bless the new lovers on their wedding night.

3. Who does Puck address at the play's end?
    He talks to the audience.

4. What is the purpose of this last speech?
    It closes the play and thanks the audience, asking that they enjoy or else pardon a frivolous entertainment.

MULTIPLE CHOICE STUDY GUIDE/QUIZ QUESTIONS - *A Midsummer Night's Dream*

Act I

1. What are Theseus and Hippolyta discussing at the play's start?
    A. They are planning a party for the King.
    B. They are discussing their wedding, which is supposed to take place in four days' time.
    C. They are debating politics.
    D. They are discussing the relative merits of the different gods.

2. How does Hippolyta come to be betrothed to Theseus?
    A. He has defeated her in battle and won her hand in marriage as a peace settlement or perhaps as the spoils of victory.
    B. Their fathers made an agreement at their births that they would marry.
    C. Theseus kidnapped her as revenge against her father.
    D. They had both received messages from Aphrodite, saying that they should wed.

3. Why is Egeus disturbed?
    A. He thinks he is paying too much in dowry offerings.
    B. He wanted to be named assistant to Theseus.
    C. His wife is angry and is threatening to leave him.
    D. He wants his daughter, Hermia, to marry Demetrius, but she loves and desires to marry Lysander.

4. What will be Hermia's fate if she refuses to marry Demetrius?
    A. She will become a servant in her father's house.
    B. She will be banished to the wilderness.
    C. She will have to choose to die or live as a cloistered nun.
    D. She will be blinded and driven off to live as a beggar.

5. To what do Lysander and Hermia agree?
    A. They will meet on the next night in the woods and escape to Lysander's aunt's house to be married.
    B. She will do as her father asks, but poison Demetrius soon after the marriage. Then she will marry Lysander.
    C. They will stand together and defy her father.
    D. They will go to the temple, make offerings to the gods, and ask for their help.

6. What hope does Helena have by telling Demetrius of Lysander and Hermia's flight?
    A. She is jealous and wants to get Hermia in as much trouble as possible.
    B. She anticipates the sweet pain of following him to and from the appointed wood while he pursues Hermia.
    C. She expects a monetary reward from Egeus for stopping Hermia.
    D. She wants Lysander to marry her instead.

A Midsummer Night's Dream Multiple Choice Study Questions Page 2

7. Who are the characters in scene two, and what do they plan?
    A. They are wedding guests, planning what to wear and where to sit.
    B. They are the bride's friends, planning what kind of gifts to give her.
    C. They are thieves, planning to rob everyone at the wedding.
    D. They are six craftsmen of Athens who plan to perform the tragedy of Pyramus and Thisby as an entertainment to honor the duke's wedding day.

A Midsummer Night's Dream Multiple Choice Study Questions Page 3

Act II

8. Why is Oberon angry with his queen?
    A. She keeps a young boy as her attendant, and Oberon wants the boy for himself. She refuses to share the child.
    B. She has much more money than he does, and will not give him the sum he wants to have available to use for his own entertainment.
    C. She has a book of spells that he wants to use, but she won't let him use it.
    D. She has recently put two of his companions in jail for mischievous conduct. He has asked her to release them, but she has refused.

9. On what mission does Oberon send Puck?
    A. Oberon sends Puck to find the parents of the young boy so they can rescue him.
    B. Oberon sends Puck to destroy the wedding feast by causing a great storm.
    C. Oberon sends Puck to find a flower that has been struck by Cupid's arrow, so he may anoint the sleeping Titania, causing her to blindly fall in love with the first creature she sees upon awakening.
    D. Oberon sends Puck to beg the queen to hear his requests.

10. Upon overhearing Demetrius and Helena, what does Oberon command Puck to do?
    A. Oberon commands Puck to send a message to Helena's father and tell him of her plan.
    B. Oberon sends Puck to make them have dreams about what the other will look like in forty years, so they will not want to marry each other.
    C. He sends Puck to cause a terrible storm that will force them to abandon their plan and return home.
    D. He sends Puck to anoint the boy's eyes as he sleeps so that upon waking he will see the maid and love her.

11. Upon whose eyes does Puck apply the potion?
    A. He does Hermia's eyes.
    B. He does Demetrius' eyes.
    C. He does Lysander's eyes.
    D. He does Egeus' eyes.

12. When he wakes up, who does Lysander see and love?
    A. He sees and loves Titania.
    B. He sees and loves Helena.
    C. He sees and loves Hermia.
    D. He sees and loves Hippolyta.

A Midsummer Night's Dream Multiple Choice Study Questions Page 4

13. What is her reaction to his words of love?
    A. She thinks he is teasing her cruelly.
    B. She believes him and falls in love with him.
    C. She thinks he has gone crazy.
    D. She thinks she is asleep and having a nightmare.

14. To where has Lysander disappeared when Hermia awakes?
    A. He has gone to follow Helena.
    B. He has gone to find Puck.
    C. He is lost in the forest.
    D. He has gone to Athens for the wedding.

A Midsummer Night's Dream Multiple Choice Study Questions Page 5

Act III

15. Why does Bottom want a prologue written for the play?
    A. He wants a prologue so he can get credit for it, and possibly more money.
    B. He wants one written so that his character can read it to the audience, assuring them no harm will cone to the actors. He thinks the ladies will swoon or panic.
    C. He wants to make the play longer so that the other actors can have more time to rob the audience.
    D. He wants to attract the attention of the queen. He hopes to become her court troubadour.

16. What has Puck done to Bottom?
    A. He has given Bottom hooves and a tail.
    B. He has changed Bottom's voice to a croak.
    C. He has changed Bottom's head into that of an ass.
    D. He has given Bottom claws for hands.

17. Identify the speaker: "Tie up my love's tongue, bring him silently."
    A. It was Helena.
    B. It was Hermia.
    C. It was Hippolyta.
    D. It was Titania.

18. What news does Puck bring Oberon?
    A. Titania is in love with a monster, and he has successfully dosed the Athenian's eyes.
    B. The child is sick and is not expected to live.
    C. Egeus is storming the woods with an army to retrieve his daughter.
    D. The players need a lot more practice before they will be ready to perform.

19. Why does Oberon send Puck to fetch Helena?
    A. He is in love with her and wants to marry her.
    B. He wants to start a fight between her and Hermia.
    C. He realizes Puck's mistake and tries to correct it by charming Demetrius to love Helena.
    D. He wants to ask her help in getting the young boy from Titania.

20. What is Helena's situation at this point in the play?
    A. She is in love with Bottom.
    B. She is loved by Lysander and Demetrius and believes they have conspired to play a cruel joke on her.
    C. She is furious at the others and threatens to leave Athens by herself.
    D. The recent events have been too much for her. She has gone home to bed.

A Midsummer Night's Dream Multiple Choice Study Questions Page 6

21. What does Helena suppose of Hermia?
    A. She thinks Hermia is an innocent bystander.
    B. She thinks Hermia has joined in the malicious pranks with the others.
    C. She thinks Hermia has been bewitched and can't help herself.
    D. She thinks Hermia has gone mad with jealousy.

22. What does Hermia think Helena has done?
    A. Hermia thinks Helena has given the young men a magic potion that has confused them.
    B. She thinks that Helena has asked for, and gotten, help from the gods.
    C. She thinks that out of jealousy Helena has made known her taller height and therefore her greater value of the two maids.
    D. Hermia thinks Helena has become afraid to die an old maid, and has decided to do anything she can to prevent that from happening.

23. Why does Oberon send Puck to confuse the two young men?
    A. They are going to fight over Helena, so Oberon has Puck lead them away from each other and to sleep.
    B. Oberon is enjoying the mischief he has caused, and he wants to see what else he can do.
    C. Oberon wants to get Puck out of the way so he can woo Helena himself.
    D. He wants to send them both back to Athens as quickly as possible.

24. What remedy corrects the crossed-loved couples?
    A. The aroma from the woods clears their senses.
    B. Puck drips the potion on Lysander's eyes so he will again love Hermia.
    C. Oberon confronts them, tells them what happened, and asks them to make their own choices.
    D. One of the craftsmen plays a love tune that secretly whispers the names of their true loves to each of them.

A Midsummer Night's Dream Multiple Choice Study Questions Page 7

Act IV

25. Why does Titania give Oberon the child?
    A. She wants to please Oberon.
    B. She regrets her selfishness and wants to make amends.
    C. Oberon has threatened her, and she does it out of fear.
    D. She no longer cares for him now that she has Bottom.

26. How does Oberon find Titania and Bottom?
    A. They are having a feast.
    B. They are playing with the child.
    C. They are asleep in each other's arms.
    D. They are preparing for their wedding.

27. Why does Oberon remove the spell he cast over the queen?
    A. He has the boy and he pities her silly new love-pet. He wants her back to her true self.
    B. It was part of the bargain he made with Puck, and he has to live up to it.
    C. He can only cast one spell at a time, and he wants to cast one on someone else now.
    D. He had a dream that the gods would punish him if he didn't remove it.

28. Finding the two couples asleep in the wood, and learning of their more balanced love, what order does Theseus give?
    A. He tells them to wait a few years until they are older, and then marry.
    B. He banishes all of them from Athens for the trouble they have caused.
    C. He orders that they should follow him and Hippolyta to be married in the temple.
    D. He orders his men to find and imprison Puck.

29. What news does Bottom bring his companions?
    A. He has a part in the entertainment but the rest don't.
    B. Their play was not well-received, and they have been asked to leave.
    C. The Duke liked them but not their play. They are to write a new play and perform again the next day.
    D. Their play has been chosen by the Duke as an entertainment. They must now get ready and meet at the palace.

A Midsummer Night's Dream Multiple Choice Study Questions Page 8

Act V

30. Why do you think Shakespeare. included a play within a play?
    A. Pyramus and Thisby is an ancient tale well known to audiences in Shakespeare's time. The audience would appreciate the jests and comments.
    B. He had been commissioned to write a play of a certain length, and his fell short. The play within a play was a filler to use up time.
    C. He uses it as a semi-veiled political speech.
    D. He used it in place of an intermission, to help refocus the audience's attention.

31. What do the fairies do after the palace goes to sleep?
    A. They go to sleep as well.
    B. Oberon sends them out to sing and dance and bless the new lovers on their wedding night.
    C. They go back to the woods to clean up the damage all of the lovers had done.
    D. They go out to play tricks on the actors.

32. Who does Puck address at the play's end?
    A. He talks to Oberon.
    B. He talks to the lovers.
    C. He talks to the playwright.
    D. He talks to the audience.

33. This last speech has many purposes. Which of these is not one of them?
    A. It closes the play.
    B. It thanks the audience.
    C. It asks that the audience enjoy or else pardon a frivolous entertainment.
    D. It reminds the audience that the actors will gladly accept monetary donations after the play.

ANSWER KEY - MULTIPLE CHOICE STUDY/QUIZ QUESTIONS
A Midsummer Night's Dream

Act One		Act Two		Act Three	
1.	B	8.	A	15.	B
2.	A	9.	C	16.	C
3.	D	10.	D	17.	D
4.	C	11.	C	18.	A
5.	A	12.	B	19.	C
6.	B	13.	A	20.	B
7.	D	14.	A	21.	B
				22.	C
				23.	A
				24.	B

Act Four		Act Five	
25.	D	30.	A
26.	C	31.	B
27.	A	32.	D
28.	C	33.	D
29.	D		

PREREADING VOCABULARY WORKSHEETS

VOCABULARY - *A Midsummer Night's Dream*

<u>Act I</u> Part I: Using Prior Knowledge and Contextual Clues

    Below are the sentences in which the vocabulary words appear in the text. Read the sentence. Use any clues you can find in the sentence combined with your prior knowledge, and write what you think the underlined words mean on the lines provided.

1. With cunning has thou <u>filched</u> my daughter's heart,
   Turned her obedience, which is due to me,
   To stubborn harshness.

   _____

2. Either to die the death, or to <u>abjure</u>
   Forever the society of men.

   _____

3. A good <u>persuasion</u>.

   _____

4. I have a widow aunt, a dowager
   Of great <u>revenue</u>, and she hath no child.

   _____

5. Tomorrow night, when Phoebe doth behold
   Her silver <u>visage</u> in the watery glass,
   Decking with liquid pearl the bladed grass,
   A time that lovers' flights doth still conceal,
   Through Athens' gates have we devised to steal.

   _____

6. Things <u>base</u> and vile, holding not quantity,
   Love can transpose to form and dignity.

   _____

Midsummer Night's Dream Prereading Vocabulary Worksheet page 2

7. So the boy Love is <u>perjured</u> everywhere:
   For ere Demetrius looked on Hermia's eyne,
   He hailed down oaths that he was only mine;

   _____

8. Marry, our play is The most <u>lamentable</u> comedy, and most cruel death of Pyramus and Thisby.

   _____

9. You may do it <u>extempore</u>, for it is nothing but roaring.

   _____

10. I grant you, friends, if you should fright the ladies out of their wits, they would have no more <u>discretion</u> but to hang us.

    _____

Act I - Part II: Determining the Meaning

You have tried to figure out the meanings of the vocabulary words for Act One. Now match the vocabulary words to their dictionary definitions. If there are words for which you cannot figure out the definition by contextual clues and by process of elimination, look them up in a dictionary.

___ 1. filched   A. face; appearance
___ 2. abjure   B. to give up; abstain from
___ 3. persuasion   C. a strongly held opinion, a conviction
___ 4. revenue   D. worthy of grief, mourning or regret
___ 5. visage   E. spoken, carried out, or composed with little or no
                          preparation or forethought
___ 6. base   F. ability or power to decide responsibly
___ 7. perjured   G. testified falsely under oath; falsified; untrue
___ 8. lamentable   H. income; wealth
___ 9. extempore   I. snitched; stole
___10. discretion   J. the lowest or bottom part

Vocabulary - *A Midsummer Night's Dream* Act II

Part I: Using Prior Knowledge and Contextual Clues

    Below are the sentences in which the vocabulary words appear in the text. Read the sentence. Use any clues you can find in the sentence combined with your prior knowledge, and write what you think the underlined words mean on the lines provided.

1. But she perforce withholds the loved boy,
   Crowns him with flowers, and makes him all her joy.

   _____

2. Playing on pipes of corn, and versing love
   To amorous Phillida.

   _____

3. For lack of tread, are undistinguishable.

   _____

4. Therefore the moon, the governess of floods,
   Pale in her anger, washes all the air,
   That rheumatic diseases do abound.

   _____

5. And on old Hiems' thin and icy crown
   An odorous chaplet of sweet summer buds
   Is, as in mockery, set.

   _____

6. Since once I sat upon a promontory
   And heard a mermaid, on dolphin's back,

   _____

Midsummer Night's Dream Prereading Vocabulary Worksheet page 4

7 Uttering such <u>dulcet</u> and harmonious breath
   That the rude sea grew civil at her song

_____

8. Use me but as your spaniel, <u>spurn</u> me, strike me,
   Neglect me, lose me---only give me leave,
   Unworthy as I am, to follow you.

_____

9. ...and some keep back
   The <u>clamorous</u> owl that nightly hoots and wonders
   At our quaint spirits.

_____

10. But you must <u>flout</u> my insufficiency?

_____

Act II - Part II: Determining the Meaning

You have tried to figure out the meanings of the vocabulary words for <u>Act Two</u>. Now match the vocabulary words to their dictionary definitions. If there are words for which you cannot figure out the definition by contextual clues and by process of elimination, look them up in a dictionary.

___ 11. perforce   A. a wreath or garland for the head
___ 12. amorous   B. to shown contempt for
___ 13. undistinguishable   C. noisy
___ 14. rheumatic   D. a high ridge of land or rock jutting out into a body of water
___ 15. chaplet   E. by necessity; by force of circumstance
___ 16. promontory   F. of, relating to, or suffering from aches in the muscles, joints or
                                 bones
___ 17. dulcet   G. strongly attracted or disposed to love
___ 18. spurn   H. pleasing to the ear; melodious
___ 19. clamorous   I. having no unique markings; can't be clearly seen
___ 20. flout   J. to kick at or tread on disdainfully

Vocabulary - *A Midsummer Night's Dream* Act III

Part I: Using Prior Knowledge and Contextual Clues

Below are the sentences in which the vocabulary words appear in the text. Read the sentence. Use any clues you can find in the sentence combined with your prior knowledge, and write what you think the underlined words mean on the lines provided.

1. We must have a wall in the great chamber, for Pyramus and Thisby, says the story, did talk through the chink of a wall.

   _____

2. When you have spoken our speech, enter into that brake.

   _____

3. This is a knavery of them to make me afeard.

   _____

4. Mine ear is much enamored of thy shape.

   _____

5. And I will purge thy mortal grossness so
   That thou shalt like an airy spirit go.

   _____

6. I promise you your kindred hath made my eyes water ere now.

   _____

7. Come, wait upon him; lead him to my bower.

   _____

8. And when she weeps, weeps every little flower,
   Lamenting some enforced chastity.

   _____

Midsummer Night's Dream Prereading Vocabulary Worksheet page 6

9. Near to her close and <u>consecrated</u> bower,
   While she was in her dull and sleeping hour,
   A crew of patches, rude mechanicals
   That work for bread upon Athenian stalls
   Were met together to rehearse a play
   Intended for great Theseus' nuptial day.

   _____

10. Oh, why <u>rebuke</u> you him that loves you so?
    Lay breath so bitter on your bitter foe.

    _____

Act III - Part II: Determining the Meaning

You have tried to figure out the meanings of the vocabulary words for Act III. Now match the vocabulary words to their dictionary definitions. If there are words for which you cannot figure out the definition by contextual clues and by process of elimination, look them up in a dictionary.

___ 21. chink   A. a woman's private chamber
___ 22. brake   B. unprincipled; crafty
___ 23. knavery   C. a thicket
___ 24. enamored   D. sacred
___ 25. purge   E. regretting deeply; mourning, expressly sorrow
___ 26. kindred   F. to criticize or reprove sharply; reprimand
___ 27. bower   G. a narrow opening, such as a crack or fissur
___ 28. lamenting   H. to remove (impurities) by or as if by cleansing
___ 29. consecrated   I. inspired with love; captivated
___ 30. rebuke   J. relatives

Vocabulary - *A Midsummer Night's Dream* Act IV

Part I: Using Prior Knowledge and Contextual Clues
    Below are the sentences in which the vocabulary words appear in the text. Read the sentence. Use any clues you can find in the sentence combined with your prior knowledge, and write what you think the underlined words mean on the lines provided.

1. Come, sit thee down upon this flowery bed,
   While I thy amiable cheeks do coy,
   And stick musk roses in thy sleek smooth head,
   And kiss thy fair large ear, my gentle joy.

   _____

2. Do not fret yourself too much in the action, monsieur, and good monsieur, have a care the honey bag break not.

   _____

3. I would be loath to have you overflown with a honey bag, signior.

   _____

4. Gently entwist, the female ivy so
   Enrings the barky fingers of the elm.

   _____

5. Her dotage now I do begin to pity.

   _____

6. I did upbraid her, and fall out with her;

   _____

7. We will, fair Queen, up to the mountain's top.
   And mark the musical confusion
   Of hounds and echo in conjunction.

   _____

Midsummer Night's Dream Prereading Vocabulary Worksheet page 8

8. How comes this gentle concord in the world,
   That hatred is so far from jealousy,
   To sleep by hate, and fear no <u>enmity</u>?

_____

9. Let's follow him,
   And by the way let us <u>recount</u> our dreams.

_____

10. Masters, I am to <u>discourse</u> wonders.

_____

Act IV - Part II: Determining the Meaning
    You have tried to figure out the meanings of the vocabulary words for Act IV. Now match the vocabulary words to their dictionary definitions. If there are words for which you cannot figure out the definition by contextual clues and by process of elimination, look them up in a dictionary.

___ 31. amiable   A. be unwilling or reluctant; disinclined.
___ 32. fret   B. twist together
___ 33. loath   C. friendly and agreeable in disposition; good-natured and likable.
___ 34. entwist   D. worry
___ 35. dotage   E. to reprove sharply; reproach.
___ 36. upbraid   F. a deterioration of mental faculties; senility
___ 37. conjunction   G. verbal expression in speech or writing
___ 38. enmity   H. to narrate the facts or particulars of
___ 39. recount   I. deep-seated, often mutual hatred.
___ 40. discourse   J. a joint or simultaneous occurrence; concurrence.

Vocabulary - *A Midsummer Night's Dream* Act V

Part I: Using Prior Knowledge and Contextual Clues
      Below are the sentences in which the vocabulary words appear in the text. Read the sentence. Use any clues you can find in the sentence combined with your prior knowledge, and write what you think the underlined words mean on the lines provided.

1. Where is our usual manager of mirth?

   _____

2. And in the modesty of fearful duty
   I read as much as from the rattling tongue
   Of saucy and audacious eloquence.

   _____

3. He bravely broached his boiling bloody breast.

   _____

4. And Thisby, tarrying in mulberry shade,
   His dagger drew, and died.

   _____

5. Not so, my lord, for his valor cannot carry his discretion, and the fox carries the goose.

   _____

6. It appears, by his small light of discretion, that he is in the wane.

   _____

7. This palpable-gross play hath well beguiled
   The heavy gait of night.

   _____

45

Midsummer Night's Dream Prereading Vocabulary Worksheet page 10

8. Now the wasted brands do glow,
   Whilst the screech owl, screeching loud,
   Puts the wretch that lies in woe
   In remembrance of a <u>shroud</u>.

   _____

9. Now it is the time of night
   That the graves, all gaping wide,
   Every one lets forth his <u>sprite</u>
   In the churchway paths to glide.

   _____

Act V - Part II: Determining the Meaning

     You have tried to figure out the meanings of the vocabulary words for Act V. Now match the vocabulary words to their dictionary definitions. If there are words for which you cannot figure out the definition by contextual clues and by process of elimination, look them up in a dictionary.

___ 41. mirth		A. a period of decline or decrease.
___ 42. audacious		B. a cloth used to wrap a body for burial
___ 43. broached		C. gladness and gaiety, especially when expressed by laughter.
___ 44. tarrying		D. bold, insolent, spirited or original
___ 45. valor		E. deluded; cheated; diverted
___ 46. wane		F. pierced in order to draw off liquid.
___ 47. beguiled		G. a specter or ghost; a soul.
___ 48. shroud		H. remaining or staying temporarily
___ 49. sprite		I. courage and boldness, as in battle; bravery

ANSWER KEY - VOCABULARY
A Midsummer Night's Dream

<u>Act I</u>
1. I
2. B
3. C
4. H
5. A
6. J
7. G
8. D
9. E
10. F

<u>Act II</u>
11. E
12. G
13. I
14. F
15. A
16. D
17. H
18. J
19. C
20. B

<u>Act III</u>
21. G
22. C
23. B
24. I
25. H
26. J
27. A
28. E
29. D
30. F

<u>Act IV</u>
31. C
32. D
33. A
34. B
35. F
36. E
37. J
38. I
39. H
40. G

<u>Act V</u>
41. C
42. D
43. F
44. H
45. I
46. A
47. E
48. B
49. G

DAILY LESSONS

LESSON ONE

Objectives
    1. To give students some background about comedy/humor in drama, literature, radio, television and movies
    2. To give students the opportunity to fulfill their nonfiction reading assignment
    3. To give students practice using the resources in the library
    4. To distribute the materials which will be used in the unit

Activity #1
    Distribute the materials which will be used in this unit. Explain in detail how students are to use these materials.

    Study Guides Students should read the study guide questions for each reading assignment prior to beginning the reading assignment to get a feeling for what events and ideas are important in the section they are about to read. After reading the section, students will (as a class or individually) answer the questions to review the important events and ideas from that section of the play. Students should keep the study guides as study materials for the unit test.

    Vocabulary Prior to reading a reading assignment, students will do vocabulary work related to the section of the play they are about to read. Following the completion of the reading of the play, there will be a vocabulary review of all the words used in the vocabulary assignments. Students should keep their vocabulary work as study materials for the unit test.

    Reading Assignment Sheet You need to fill in the reading assignment sheet to let students know by when their reading has to be completed. You can either write the assignment sheet up on a side blackboard or bulletin board and leave it there for students to see each day, or you can "ditto" copies for each student to have. In either case, you should advise students to become very familiar with the reading assignments so they know what is expected.

    Extra Activities Center The Unit Resource portion of this unit contains suggestions for an extra library of related plays and articles in your classroom as well as crossword and word search puzzles. Make an extra activities center in your room where you will keep these materials for students to use. (Bring the books and articles in from the library and keep several copies of the puzzles on hand.) Explain to students that these materials are available for students to use when they finish reading assignments or other class work early.

    Nonfiction Assignment Sheet Explain to students that they each are to read at least one nonfiction piece from the in-class library at some time during the unit. Students will fill out a nonfiction assignment sheet after completing the reading to help you (the teacher) evaluate their reading experiences and to help the students think about and evaluate their own reading experiences.

Activity #2
    Take students to your school library. Distribute the Research Assignment Sheet. Discuss the directions in detail, and give students ample time to complete the assignment.

RESEARCH ASSIGNMENT - *Midsummer Night's Dream*

Purposes
1. To give you some background information about comedy and humor
2. To help you fulfill the nonfiction reading assignment which is a part of this unit
3. To show you that there are different kinds of humor and different ways comedy/humor is expressed

Assignment

Use the resources of your library and/or media center to find out as much as you can about the topic your group has been assigned. Take notes so you remember what you have read, seen or heard. After you have collected your information, get together with the other members of your group to compile a "Fact Sheet," an outline of the facts you have gathered. You will be asked to give an oral report to share your information with the rest of your classmates so that everyone in your class will have information about each of the topics assigned. The "Fact Sheet" you prepare will be the basis of your oral report and, if duplicated, will serve as a study guide for you and your classmates. Feel free to use audio or video clips during your reports as well.

If you wish, you may use this assignment to fulfill your nonfiction reading assignment for this unit. If you choose to do so, be sure to fill out your Nonfiction Reading Assignment Sheet.

Group 1: Kinds of Comedy/Humor. Your job is to research and find out what the different kinds of comedy/humor are. What are the main characteristics of each type? Give a couple of examples of each type of comedy/humor.

Group 2: Shakespearian Comedies. Your job is to research and find out what kinds of comedies Shakespeare wrote. What are the main characteristics of Shakespeare's comedies? Give examples from his works.

Group 3: History of Comedy in Drama. Your job is to research and find out where comedy in drama began and to trace its history to the present day. Give examples.

Group 4: History of Comedy in Radio/TV/Movies. In modern times, radio, television and the movies have all been sources of comedy. Your job is to trace the history of comedy in radio, television and the movies. Give examples.

Group 5: Uses of Comedy. Your job is to find out how and why people use and like comedy. Give specific examples.

Group 6: Great Comic Characters in Drama/Literature. Your job is to tell about some of the greatest comic characters in all of Drama and Literature through the years. Choose at least ten of the most outstanding characters. Identify them, tell what kind of comedy/humor they used, and give some of their classic examples.

Group 7: Great Comic Characters in Radio/TV/Movies. Your job is to tell about some of the greatest comic characters in all of Radio, TV and the Movies through the years. Choose at least ten of the most outstanding characters. Identify them, tell what kind of comedy/humor they used, and give some of their classic examples.

NONFICTION ASSIGNMENT SHEET - *Midsummer Night's Dream*
(To be completed after reading the required nonfiction article)

Name _____ Date _____

Title of Nonfiction Read _____

Written By _____ Publication Date _____

I. Factual Summary: Write a short summary of the piece you read.

II. Vocabulary
    1. With which vocabulary words in the piece did you encounter some degree of difficulty?

    2. How did you resolve your lack of understanding with these words?

III. Interpretation: What was the main point the author wanted you to get from reading his work?

IV. Criticism
    1. With which points of the piece did you agree or find easy to accept? Why?

    2. With which points of the piece did you disagree or find difficult to believe? Why?

V. Personal Response: What do you think about this piece? <u>OR</u> How does this piece influence your ideas?

LESSON TWO

Objectives
    1. To give students time to finish their research
    2. To give students time to compile their fact sheets
    3. To evaluate students' research
    4. To have students share all the information they have found

Activity #1
    Give students ample time to complete their research and compile their research fact sheets.

Activity #2
    Have one student from each group give an oral report to the class summarizing the information all the group members found. If you choose, students could just listen instead of taking notes, and you could duplicate the fact sheets for distribution in the next class period. The other alternative is to have students take notes from the class reports so they have study materials.

LESSON THREE

Objectives
1. To assign reading parts for Act I
2. To do the prereading activities for Act I

Activity #1

Explain that because *Midsummer Night's Dream* is a play it is meant to be acted on a stage. If you are not planning a production of the play, explain to students that the next best thing we can do is to read the parts orally. Each person in class will (eventually) have a speaking part to perform. The part does not have to be memorized, but the students' oral reading will be evaluated.

Make the reading part assignments for Act I, which will be read in Lessons Four and Five.
Narrator (stage descriptions and directions; italicized)

Theseus	Hippolyta
Philostrate	Egeus
Hermia	Lysander
Demetrius	Helena
Bottom	Flute
Snout	Quince
Starveling	Snug

Activity #3

Prior to reading Act I, students should preview the study questions and do the prereading vocabulary work for Act I. Give students the remainder of this class period to do the prereading work and, if they finish that, to begin practicing their oral reading parts.

LESSONS FOUR AND FIVE

Objectives
1. To read Act I of *Midsummer Night's Dream*
2. To evaluate students' oral reading

Activity

Have students who were assigned to read parts for Act I do so during these class periods. If you have not yet evaluated students' oral reading this marking period, this would be a good opportunity to do so. An Oral Reading Evaluation form is included in this unit for your convenience.

LESSON SIX

Objectives
1. To review the main events and ideas presented in Act I
2. To assign the speaking parts for Act II
3. To do the prereading work for Act II

Activity #1

Give students a few minutes to formulate answers for the study guide questions for Act I, and then discuss the answers to the questions in detail. Write the answers on the board or overhead transparency so students can have the correct answers for study purposes. Note: It is a good practice in public speaking and leadership skills for individual students to take charge of leading the discussions of the study questions. Perhaps a different student could go to the front of the class and lead the discussion each day that the study questions are discussed during this unit. Of course, the teacher should guide the discussion when appropriate and be sure to fill in any gaps the students leave.

Activity #2

Assign the following speaking parts for Act II. (Tell students that they will be reading Act II during the next class period.)

Narrator	Puck
Fairy 1	Oberon
Titania	Demetrius
Helena	Fairy 2
Lysander	Hermia

Activity #3

Prior to reading Act II, students should preview the study questions and do the prereading vocabulary work for Act II. Give students the remainder of this class period to do the prereading work and, if they finish that, to begin practicing their oral reading parts.

ORAL READING EVALUATION - *A Midsummer Night's Dream*

Name _____ Class _____ Date _____

SKILL	EXCELLENT	GOOD	AVERAGE	FAIR	POOR
Fluency	5	4	3	2	1
Clarity	5	4	3	2	1
Audibility	5	4	3	2	1
Pronunciation	5	4	3	2	1
_____	5	4	3	2	1
_____	5	4	3	2	1

Total _____ Grade _____

Comments:

LESSON SEVEN

Objectives
    1. To read Act II of *Midsummer Night's Dream*
    2. To evaluate students' oral reading

Activity
    Have students who were assigned to read parts for Act I do so during these class periods. If you have not yet evaluated students' oral reading this marking period, this would be a good opportunity to do so. An Oral Reading Evaluation form is included in this unit for your convenience.

LESSON EIGHT

Objectives
    1. To give students practice writing to inform
    2. To review
    3. To give the teacher the opportunity to evaluate students' writing

Activity
    Distribute Writing Assignment 1. Discuss the directions in detail and give students this class period to do the assignment.

    Follow - Up: After you have graded the assignments, have a writing conference with the students. After the writing conference, allow students to revise their papers using your suggestions and corrections. Give them about three days from the date they receive their papers to complete the revision. I suggest grading the revisions on an A-C-E scale (all revisions well-done, some revisions made, few or no revisions made). This will speed your grading time and still give some credit for the students' efforts.

WRITING ASSIGNMENT #1 - *Midsummer Night's Dream*

PROMPT
Your assignment is to write a complete composition about the background information you researched at the beginning of this unit.

PREWRITING
Start by looking at the notes you took as you were gathering information. Then, look at the fact sheet you and the members of your group compiled. Think of one statement you could make about all this information. That will be the main idea of your paper. Can the information you have gathered be put into categories? (Are there some things that naturally go together?) Is there a logical progression of ideas? (Can your information be put in chronological order? If so, do it.)

DRAFTING
First write a paragraph in which you introduce the topic of your composition. The paragraphs in the body of your composition will all support or explain your main topic. The paragraphs should flow from idea to idea (from category to category, or in chronological order from earliest to latest, etc.). Your final paragraph should include the conclusions you can draw from the information presented and should bring your composition to a close.

PROMPT
When you finish the rough draft of your paper, ask a student who sits near you to read it. After reading your rough draft, he/she should tell you what he/she liked best about your work, which parts were difficult to understand, and ways in which your work could be improved. Reread your paper considering your critic's comments, and make the corrections you think are necessary.

PROOFREADING
Do a final proofreading of your paper double-checking your grammar, spelling, organization, and the clarity of your ideas.

LESSON NINE

Objectives
1. To review the main events and ideas presented in Act II
2. To assign the speaking parts for Act III
3. To do the prereading work for Act III

Activity #1
Give students a few minutes to formulate answers for the study guide questions for Act II, and then discuss the answers to the questions in detail. Write the answers on the board or overhead transparency so students can have the correct answers for study purposes.

Activity #2
Assign the following speaking parts for Act III. (Tell students that they will be reading Act III during the next class period.)

Narrator	Bottom
Quince	Snout
Starveling	Snug
Puck	Titania
Fairies	Hermia
Helena	Oberon
Demetrius	Lysander
	Cobweb, Peasblossom, Mustardseed

Activity #3
Prior to reading Act III, students should preview the study questions and do the prereading vocabulary work for Act III. Give students the remainder of this class period to do the prereading work and, if they finish that, to begin practicing their oral reading parts.

LESSONS TEN AND ELEVEN

Objectives
1. To read Act III of *Midsummer Night's Dream*
2. To evaluate students' oral reading

Activity
Have students who were assigned to read parts for Act III do so during these class periods. Continue the oral reading evaluations if you have not yet given everyone in the class a grade for oral reading.

LESSON TWELVE

Objectives
    1. To review the main events and ideas presented in Act III
    2. To assign the speaking parts for Act IV
    3. To do the prereading work for Act IV

Activity #1
    Give students a few minutes to formulate answers for the study guide questions for Act III, and then discuss the answers to the questions in detail. Write the answers on the board or overhead transparency so students can have the correct answers for study purposes.

Activity #2
    Assign the following speaking parts for Act IV. (Tell students that they will be reading Act IV during the next class period.)

Narrator	Titania
Bottom	Peasblossom, Cobweb, Mustardseed
Oberon	Puck
Theseus	Hippolyta
Egeus	Demetrius
Lysander	Hermia
Helena	Quince
Starveling	Flute
Bottom	Snug

Activity #3
    Prior to reading Act IV, students should preview the study questions and do the prereading vocabulary work for Act IV. Give students the remainder of this class period to do the prereading work and, if they finish that, to begin practicing their oral reading parts.

LESSON THIRTEEN

Objectives
    1. To read Act IV of *Midsummer Night's Dream*
    2. To evaluate students' oral reading

Activity
    Have students who were assigned to read parts for Act IV do so during these class periods. Continue the oral reading evaluations if you have not yet given everyone in the class a grade for oral reading.

LESSON FOURTEEN

Objectives
1. To review the main events and ideas presented in Act IV
2. To assign the speaking parts for Act V
3. To do the prereading work for Act V

Activity #1
Give students a few minutes to formulate answers for the study guide questions for Act IV, and then discuss the answers to the questions in detail. Write the answers on the board or overhead transparency so students can have the correct answers for study purposes.

Activity #2
Assign the following speaking parts for Act V. (Tell students that they will be reading Act V during the next class period.)

Narrator	Hippolyta
Theseus	Lysander
Philostrate	Prologue
Demetrius	Wall
Pyramus	Thisby
Lion	Moonshine
Bottom	Puck
Oberon	Titania

Activity #3
Prior to reading Act V, students should preview the study questions and do the prereading vocabulary work for Act V. Give students the remainder of this class period to do the prereading work and, if they finish that, to begin practicing their oral reading parts.

LESSON FIFTEEN

Objectives
1. To read Act V of *Midsummer Night's Dream*
2. To evaluate students' oral reading

Activity
Have students who were assigned to read parts for Act V do so during these class periods. Continue the oral reading evaluations if you have not yet given everyone in the class a grade for oral reading.

LESSON SIXTEEN

Objectives
    1. To review the main ideas and events from Act V
    2. To review all of the vocabulary work done in this unit

Activity #1
    Give students a few minutes to formulate answers for the study guide questions for Act V, and then discuss the answers to the questions in detail.

Activity #2
    Choose one (or more) of the vocabulary review activities listed on the next page and spend your class period as directed in the activity. Some of the materials for these review activities are located in the Extra Activities Section in this unit.

LESSON SEVENTEEN

Objectives
    1. To give students the opportunity to practice writing to persuade
    2. To give the teacher a chance to evaluate students' individual writing
    3. To give students the opportunity to correct their writing errors and produce an error-free paper

Activity
    Distribute Writing Assignment 2. Discuss the directions in detail and give students ample time to complete the assignment.

    While students are doing their writing assignments, call individuals to your desk (or some other private area) to discuss their papers from Writing Assignment 1. A Writing Evaluation Form is included with this unit to help structure your conferences.

VOCABULARY REVIEW ACTIVITIES

1. Divide your class into two teams and have an old-fashioned spelling or definition bee.

2. Give each of your students (or students in groups of two, three or four) a *Midsummer Night's Dream* Vocabulary Word Search Puzzle. The person (group) to find all of the vocabulary words in the puzzle first wins.

3. Give students a *Midsummer Night's Dream* Vocabulary Word Search Puzzle without the word list. The person or group to find the most vocabulary words in the puzzle wins.

4. Use a *Midsummer Night's Dream* Vocabulary Crossword Puzzle. Put the puzzle onto a transparency on the overhead projector (so everyone can see it), and do the puzzle together as a class.

5. Give students a *Midsummer Night's Dream* Vocabulary Matching Worksheet to do.

6. Divide your class into two teams. Use the *Midsummer Night's Dream* vocabulary words with their letters jumbled as a word list. Student 1 from Team A faces off against Student 1 from Team B. You write the first jumbled word on the board. The first student (1A or 1B) to unscramble the word wins the chance for his/her team to score points. If 1A wins the jumble, go to student 2A and give him/her a definition. He/she must give you the correct spelling of the vocabulary word which fits that definition. If he/she does, Team A scores a point, and you give student 3A a definition for which you expect a correctly spelled matching vocabulary word. Continue giving Team A definitions until some team member makes an incorrect response. An incorrect response sends the game back to the jumbled-word face off, this time with students 2A and 2B. Instead of repeating giving definitions to the first few students of each team, continue with the student after the one who gave the last incorrect response on the team. For example, if Team B wins the jumbled-word face-off, and student 5B gave the last incorrect answer for Team B, you would start this round of definition questions with student 6B, and so on. The team with the most points wins!

7. Have students write a story in which they correctly use as many vocabulary words as possible. Have students read their compositions orally! Post the most original compositions on your bulletin board!

WRITING ASSIGNMENT #2 - *Midsummer Night's Dream*

PROMPT

Humor is entertaining but it can also be useful. It can help show us good from bad and right from wrong, and it can relax us in tense situations. How many times has a guest speaker told a joke at the beginning of his speech to "break the ice." People of all ages like humor, but little kids seem to laugh especially easily at things. That makes humor an especially good way to reach kids--to put their fears at ease and to teach them things. Almost every kid goes through a stage when he/she is afraid of the dark or is afraid that a monster is going to get him/her. *Sesame Street*, for example, has taken monsters and has made them cute, furry, friendly, and funny.

Your assignment is to create a humorous puppet sketch in which you persuade a little boy or girl that there is no need to be afraid of the dark. You may use as many puppets/characters as you want, and you may make them any characters you want. Your sketch should last 3-5 minutes; kids don't have a very long attention span.

PREWRITING

Why are kids afraid of the dark? What exactly are they afraid of? Make a list of reasons why kids are afraid in the dark. Choose one or two of these fears to try to overcome in your sketch. Make some notes about in what ways you could use your puppets to persuade the little boy or girl that the dark is nothing to be afraid of. Remember, your sketch must be a humorous sketch, not just two little puppets telling each other that there is no need to be afraid in the dark. Use your imagination and creativity to really persuade your audience.

DRAFTING

Keeping your purpose in mind, make a rough draft -- a plot summary -- of your sketch. Then, go back and follow the plot summary and write in the dialogue, puppet actions, scenery, stage directions, etc.

PROMPT

When you finish the rough draft of your paper, ask a student who sits near you to read it. After reading your rough draft, he/she should tell you what he/she liked best about your work, which parts were difficult to understand, and ways in which your work could be improved. Reread your paper considering your critic's comments, and make the corrections you think are necessary.

PROOFREADING

Do a final proofreading of your paper double-checking your grammar, spelling, organization, and the clarity of your ideas.

WRITING EVALUATION FORM - *Midsummer Night's Dream*

Name _____ Date _____

Writing Assignment #1 for the *Midsummer Night's Dream* unit   Grade _____

Circle One For Each Item:

Grammar: excellent   good   fair   poor

Spelling: excellent   good   fair   poor

Punctuation: excellent   good   fair   poor

Legibility: excellent   good   fair   poor

Strengths:

Weaknesses:

Comments/Suggestions:

LESSONS EIGHTEEN AND NINETEEN

Objectives
1. To review the different kinds of humor
2. To give students the opportunity to work with humor--to write it and perform it

Activity #1

Ask students to orally give you a list of all the different kinds of humor they have learned about in this unit. Write them all on the board.

Activity #2

Divide students into groups of twos and or threes. Tell students that they will be putting on a Comic Variety Show. The show will consist of "acts" they will perform using the different kinds of humor they have learned about. Assign one type of humor to each group of students. The students are to create a short "act" based on that type of humor. Each "act" should last between three and five minutes.

Give students this class time to plan what they are going to do, write their scripts, and decide what props they will need, if any. It would be a good idea to have on hand in your classroom books of jokes, riddles, puns, limericks, etc. to help students generate ideas. Tell students that they should have their acts prepared by the day after the unit test. Give students a day/date. Invite another English class or two to see your students' performances.

LESSON TWENTY

Objectives
1. To discuss *Midsummer Night's Dream* on interpretive and critical levels
2. To take a closer look at Shakespeare's language and significant quotations from *Midsummer Night's Dream*

Activity

Choose the questions from the Extra Discussion Questions/Writing Assignments which seem most appropriate for your students. A class discussion of these questions is most effective if students have been given the opportunity to formulate answers to the questions prior to the discussion. To this end, you may either have all the students formulate answers to all the questions, divide your class into groups and assign one or more questions to each group, or you could assign one question to each student in your class. The option you choose will make a difference in the amount of class time needed for this activity.

After students have had ample time to formulate answers to the questions, begin your class discussion of the questions and the ideas presented by the questions. Be sure students take notes during the discussion so they have information to study for the unit test.

EXTRA WRITING ASSIGNMENTS/DISCUSSION QUESTIONS - *Midsummer Night's Dream*

Interpretation

1. Identify all the references to dreams and dreaming in the play.

2. What is the setting of *Midsummer Night's Dream*?

3. Where is the climax of the play? Explain your choice.

4. The language in the play is pretty straightforward. When one character likes another, the language is melodramatically sweet. Likewise, when one character does not like another, it is melodramatically harsh. Find several examples of each of these two kinds of language.

5. Think of a different title for the play. Explain your choice.

6. What are the main conflicts in the play, and how are they resolved?

Critical

7. Explain why Puck is one of Shakespeare's most memorable characters.

8. Which character is responsible for causing most of the action in the play? How?

9. Define "tragedy," "comedy," and "romance" in the literary sense of the words. Explain into what category or categories *A Midsummer Night's Dream* falls and why.

10. Evaluate William Shakespeare's style of writing. How does it contribute to the value of the play?

11. Are the characters' actions believably motivated? Why or why not?

12. Choose a passage from *A Midsummer Night's Dream* (at least 10 lines). Analyze the meter, rhymes and word choice in relationship to the meaning and action of the passage.

13. Compare and contrast the female characters in the play: Hermia, Helena, Titania, and Hippolyta.

14. What things in *A Midsummer Night's Dream* are due to supernatural powers, and what effect does that have on our perception of the play?

15. Compare and contrast the male characters in the play: Lysander, Demetrius, Oberon and Theseus.

Midsummer Night's Dream Extra Discussion Questions page 2

16. Why do we get to know the players in the "Pyramus and Thisby" play? What does our insight into their characters add to Shakespeare's play?

17. What parallels are there between "Pyramus and Thisby" and *A Midsummer Night's Dream*?

18. Why does Shakespeare have Nick Bottom inquire about the names of Titania's fairies who are his servants?

19. How does *A Midsummer Night's Dream* portray people in love? Explain your answer using examples from the text.

20. The moon is traditionally associated with couples in love. How does Shakespeare use it in this play?

21. Compare and contrast the fairies and mortals in this play.

22. Identify and explain the following quotations:
    a. "Rather your eyes must with his judgement look."
    b. "The course of true love never did run smooth."
    c. "Lord, what fools these mortals be!"
    d. "Methought I was enamour'd of an ass."
    e. "The kinder we, to give them thanks for nothing."

Critical/Personal Response
21. Which minor character is the most important to the play?

22. Would you like to have a father like Egeus? Why or why not?

23. What scenes or passages from the play would make a good "Vaudeville" act?

Personal Response
24. Did you enjoy reading *Midsummer Night's Dream*? Why or why not?

25. Do you believe in "love at first sight"? Why or why not?

26. Have you read any other stories about love at first sight or stories about fairies?

LESSON TWENTY-ONE

Objectives
1. To give students the opportunity to do some creative writing with their own ideas
2. To extend students' knowledge of the characters and events in *Midsummer Night's Dream*
3. To give the teacher a chance to evaluate students' individual writing
4. To give students the opportunity to correct their writing errors and produce an error-free paper

Activity

Distribute Writing Assignment #3. Discuss the directions orally in detail. Allow the remaining class time for students to complete the activity.

If students do not have enough class time to finish, the papers may be collected at the beginning of the next class period.

Follow-Up: Follow up as in Writing Assignment 1, allowing students to correct their errors and turn in the revision for credit. A good time for your next writing conferences would be the day following the unit test.

WRITING ASSIGNMENT #3 - *A Midsummer Night's Dream*

PROMPT

A Midsummer Night's Dream provides some fun topics for discussion. There's the whole idea about what simpletons we become when we "fall in love," the idea of "love at first sight," the notions of dreams and dreaming, and fantasies and frolics in a make-believe world. It is a very light play, entertaining, and humorous.

Here's your chance to write about a topic that interests you. Choose one of the following topics about which to write a composition expressing your own personal opinions:

1. What happens to us when we "fall in love"?
2. Do you believe in "love at first sight"?
3. Do you think dreams have any significance?
4. What was the most vivid dream you remember having?
5. Do you think there could be a world of sprites and fairies--a world of other beings we can't see--that affects our daily lives?
6. Did you think *A Midsummer Night's Dream* was funny? What made it funny for you?

PREWRITING

Decide which of the topics above you would like to choose. Make some notes about your answer(s) to the question(s) posed. Organize your thoughts/notes into a logical order.

DRAFTING

Write an introductory paragraph in which you introduce the topic of your composition.
In the body of your composition, write at least three paragraphs giving your opinions/ideas.
Write a paragraph in which you conclude your thoughts and close your composition.

PROMPT

When you finish the rough draft of your paper, ask a student who sits near you to read it. After reading your rough draft, he/she should tell you what he/she liked best about your work, which parts were difficult to understand, and ways in which your work could be improved. Reread your paper considering your critic's comments, and make the corrections you think are necessary.

PROOFREADING

Do a final proofreading of your paper double-checking your grammar, spelling, organization, and the clarity of your ideas.

LESSON TWENTY-TWO

Objectives
1. To bring the *Midsummer Night's Dream* unit to a close
2. To tie together all the ideas and analyses for the unit
3. To give students a look at the play *Midsummer Night's Dream* because plays are meant to be seen and heard and acted out

Activity

The best thing to do is to take students to see a production of *Midsummer Night's Dream*. If however, that is impossible, find a film of the play and show it to your students. Tell students to bear in mind everything they have learned about *Midsummer Night's Dream* as they view the film.

If you have students whose minds will wander instead of watching the film, tell your students to keep a little written list of things comparing and contrasting the film with your text and their expectations.

LESSON TWENTY-THREE

Objective

To review the main ideas presented in *Midsummer Night's Dream*

Activity #1

Choose one of the review games/activities included in this unit and spend your class period as outlined there. Some materials for these activities are located in the Unit Resource section of this unit.

Activity #2

Remind students that the Unit Test will be in the next class meeting. Stress the review of the Study Guides and their class notes as a last minute, brush-up review for homework.

REVIEW GAMES/ACTIVITIES - *A Midsummer Night's Dream*

1. Ask the class to make up a unit test for Midsummer Night's Dream. The test should have 4 sections: matching, true/false, short answer, and essay. Students may use 1/2 period to make the test and then swap papers and use the other 1/2 class period to take a test a classmate has devised. (open book) You may want to use the unit test included in this unit or take questions from the students' unit tests to formulate your own test.

2. Take 1/2 period for students to make up true and false questions (including the answers). Collect the papers and divide the class into two teams. Draw a big tic-tac-toe board on the chalk board. Make one team X and one team O. Ask questions to each side, giving each student one turn. If the question is answered correctly, that students' team's letter (X or O) is placed in the box. If the answer is incorrect, no mark is placed in the box. The object is to get three marks in a row like tic-tac-toe. You may want to keep track of the number of games won for each team.

3. Take 1/2 period for students to make up questions (true/false and short answer). Collect the questions. Divide the class into two teams. You'll alternate asking questions to individual members of teams A & B (like in a spelling bee). The question keeps going from A to B until it is correctly answered, then a new question is asked. A correct answer does not allow the team to get another question. Correct answers are +2 points; incorrect answers are -1 point.

4. Have students pair up and quiz each other from their study guides and class notes.

5. Give students a *Midsummer Night's Dream* crossword puzzle to complete.

6. Divide your class into two teams. Use the *Midsummer Night's Dream* crossword words with their letters jumbled as a word list. Student 1 from Team A faces off against Student 1 from Team B. You write the first jumbled word on the board. The first student (1A or 1B) to unscramble the word wins the chance for his/her team to score points. If 1A wins the jumble, go to student 2A and give him/her a clue. He/she must give you the correct word which matches that clue. If he/she does, Team A scores a point, and you give student 3A a clue for which you expect another correct response. Continue giving Team A clues until some team member makes an incorrect response. An incorrect response sends the game back to the jumbled-word face off, this time with students 2A and 2B. Instead of repeating giving clues to the first few students of each team, continue with the student after the one who gave the last incorrect response on the team. For example, if Team B wins the jumbled-word face-off, and student 5B gave the last incorrect answer for Team B, you would start this round of clue questions with student 6B, and so on. The team with the most points wins!

UNIT TESTS

SHORT ANSWER UNIT TEST 1 - *A Midsummer Night's Dream*

I. Matching/Identify

___ 1. Egeus   A. Helena loves him, but he's to marry Hermia

___ 2. Lysander   B. Queen of the Amazons

___ 3. Theseus   C. Queen of the Fairies

___ 4. Hippolyta   D. Hermia loves him

___ 5. Oberon   E. Wrote "Pyramus and Thisby"

___ 6. Helena   F. Duke of Athens

___ 7. Puck   G. Father of Hermia

___ 8. Hermia   H. Wants to play all the roles

___ 9. Titania   I. Plays Lion

___ 10. Quince   J. Robin Goodfellow

___ 11. Flute   K. Plays Wall

___ 12. Demetrius   L. Tells Hermia's plans to Demetrius

___ 13. Bottom   M. Plays Thisby

___ 14. Snout   N. Arranges to meet Lysander in the woods

___ 15. Snug   O. King of the Fairies

Midsummer Night's Dream Short Answer Unit Test 1 page 2

II. Short Answer

1. What are Theseus and Hippolyta discussing at the play's start?

2. What does Oberon send Puck to do to Titania?

3. Upon overhearing Demetrius and Helena, what does Oberon command Puck to do?

4. When he wakes up, who does Lysander see and love?

5. Why does Bottom want a prologue written for the play?

6. What has Puck done to Bottom?

7. What remedy corrects the crossed-loved couples?

A Midsummer Night's Dream Short Answer Unit Test 1

8. Why does Oberon remove the spell he has cast over his queen?

9. Finding the two couples asleep in the wood and learning of their more balanced love, what order does Theseus give?

10. What do the fairies do after the palace goes to sleep?

III. Composition

What elements in Shakespeare's play *A Midsummer Night's Dream* make it one of his most popular comedies?

A Midsummer Night's Dream Short Answer Unit Test 1 Page 4

IV. Vocabulary

Listen to the vocabulary words and write them down. Go back later and fill in the correct definition for each word.

1.

2.

3.

4.

5.

6.

7.

8.

9.

10.

KEY: SHORT ANSWER UNIT TEST #1 - *A Midsummer Night's Dream*

I. Matching/Identify

_G_	1. Egeus	A. Helena loves him, but he's to marry Hermia
_D_	2. Lysander	B. Queen of the Amazons
_F_	3. Theseus	C. Queen of the Fairies
_B_	4. Hippolyta	D. Hermia loves him
_O_	5. Oberon	E. Wrote "Pyramus and Thisby"
_L_	6. Helena	F. Duke of Athens
_J_	7. Puck	G. Father of Hermia
_N_	8. Hermia	H. Wants to play all the roles
_C_	9. Titania	I. Plays Lion
_E_	10. Quince	J. Robin Goodfellow
_M_	11. Flute	K. Plays Wall
_A_	12. Demetrius	L. Tells Hermia's plans to Demetrius
_H_	13. Bottom	M. Plays Thisby
_K_	14. Snout	N. Arranges to meet Lysander in the woods
_I_	15. Snug	O. King of the Fairies

II. Short Answer

1. What are Theseus and Hippolyta discussing at the play's start?
   They are discussing their wedding which is supposed to take place in four days' time.
2. What does Oberon send Puck to do to Titania?
   Oberon sends Puck to find a flower that has been struck by Cupid's arrow so that he may anoint the sleeping Titania, causing her to blindly love the first creature she sees upon awaking.

3. Upon overhearing Demetrius and Helena, what does Oberon command Puck to do?

   He tells Puck to find the Athenian couple and anoint the youth's eyes as he sleeps so that upon waking he will see the maid and love her.

4. When he wakes up, who does Lysander see and love?

   He sees Helena.

5. Why does Bottom want a prologue written for the play?

   He wants one written so that his character can read it to the audience, assuring them that no harm will come to the actors either by sword or by lion. He thinks the ladies will go into a swoon or else panic.

6. What has Puck done to Bottom?

   He has changed his head into that of an ass.

7. What remedy corrects the crossed-loved couples?

   Puck drips the potion on Lysander's eyes so he will love his former sweetheart, Hermia. He leaves Demetrius loving Helena.

8. Why does Oberon remove the spell he has cast over his queen?

   He has the boy and now he pities his queen her silly new love-pet. He wants her back to her true self.

9. Finding the two couples asleep in the wood and learning of their more balanced love, what order does Theseus give?

   He orders that they should follow him and Hippolyta to be married with them at the temple.

10. What do the fairies do after the palace goes to sleep?

    Oberon sends them off throughout the house to sing and dance and bless the new lovers on their wedding night.

III. Composition   Answers will vary.

   What elements in Shakespeare's play *A Midsummer Night's Dream* make it one of his most popular comedies?

IV. Vocabulary

   Choose ten of the vocabulary words. Read them orally to your class so the students can write them down on part IV of their vocabulary tests.

SHORT ANSWER UNIT TEST 2 - *A Midsummer Night's Dream*

I. Matching/Identify

___ 1. Egeus   A. Duke of Athens

___ 2. Lysander   B. Wants to play all the roles

___ 3. Theseus   C. Queen of the Fairies

___ 4. Hippolyta   D. Father of Hermia

___ 5. Oberon   E. Wrote "Pyramus and Thisby"

___ 6. Helena   F. Helena loves him, but he's to marry Hermia

___ 7. Puck   G. Hermia loves him

___ 8. Hermia   H. Plays Wall

___ 9. Titania   I. Robin Goodfellow

___ 10. Quince   J. Plays Lion

___ 11. Flute   K. Queen of the Amazons

___ 12. Demetrius   L. Plays Thisby

___ 13. Bottom   M. Tells Hermia's plans to Demetrius

___ 14. Snout   N. King of the Fairies

___ 15. Snug   O. Arranges to meet Lysander in the woods

II. Short Answer

1. To what do Lysander and Hermia agree?

Midsummer Night's Dream Short Answer Unit Test 2 page 2

2. What hope does Helena have by telling Demetrius of Lysander and Hermia's flight?

3. On what mission does Oberon send Puck?

4. Upon whose eyes does Puck apply the potion?

5. When he wakes up, who does Lysander see and love?

6. Why does Oberon send Puck to fetch Helena?

7. Why does Oberon send Puck to confuse the two young men?

8. What remedy corrects the crossed-loved couples?

9. Finding the two couples asleep in the wood and learning of their more balanced love, what order does Theseus give?

Midsummer Night's Dream Short Answer Unit Test 2 page 3

10. Why do you think Shakespeare included a play within a play?

11. What is the purpose of Puck's last speech?

III. Composition
    Discuss two different kinds of humor Shakespeare uses in *A Midsummer Night's Dream*. Use specific examples from the text to support your statements.

Midsummer Night's Dream Short Answer Unit Test 2 page 4

IV. Vocabulary

Listen to the vocabulary words and write them down. Go back later and fill in the correct definition for each word.

1.

2.

3.

4.

5.

6.

7.

8.

9.

10.

KEY: SHORT ANSWER UNIT TEST 2 *A Midsummer Night's Dream*

I. Matching (Use this matching key also for the Advanced Short Answer Unit Test)

_D_	1. Egeus	A. Duke of Athens
_G_	2. Lysander	B. Wants to play all the roles
_A_	3. Theseus	C. Queen of the Fairies
_K_	4. Hippolyta	D. Father of Hermia
_N_	5. Oberon	E. Wrote "Pyramus and Thisby"
_M_	6. Helena	F. Helena loves him, but he's to marry Hermia
_I_	7. Puck	G. Hermia loves him
_O_	8. Hermia	H. Plays Wall
_C_	9. Titania	I. Robin Goodfellow
_E_	10. Quince	J. Plays Lion
_L_	11. Flute	K. Queen of the Amazons
_F_	12. Demetrius	L. Plays Thisby
_B_	13. Bottom	M. Tells Hermia's plans to Demetrius
_H_	14. Snout	N. King of the Fairies
_J_	15. Snug	O. Arranges to meet Lysander in the woods

II. Short Answer

1. To what do Lysander and Hermia agree?

   They agree to meet on the next night in a wood a league from Athens and from there to make their way to the remote home of Lysander's aunt where they can be married and safe from Athen's cruel punishment and separation.

2. What hope does Helena have by telling Demetrius of Lysander and Hermia's flight?
    She anticipates the sweet pain of following him to and from the appointed wood while he pursues Hermia.
3. On what mission does Oberon send Puck?
    Oberon sends Puck to find a flower that has been struck by Cupid's arrow so that he may anoint the sleeping Titania, causing her to blindly love the first creature she sees upon awaking.
4. Upon whose eyes does Puck apply the potion?
    He does Lysander's eyes by mistake.
5. When he wakes up, who does Lysander see and love?
    He sees Helena.
6. Why does Oberon send Puck to fetch Helena?
    He realizes that another Athenian youth was dosed by Puck by mistake and that now a maid has lost her true love (Lysander) and the intended youth (Demetrius) is still repulsing Helena. While Puck is away, Oberon charms Demetrius to love Helena when he sees her again.
7. Why does Oberon send Puck to confuse the two young men?
    They are going to fight over Helena, so Oberon has Puck make the night darken and cloudy and use his voice to lead them away from each other and to sleep.
8. What remedy corrects the crossed-loved couples?
    Puck drips the potion on Lysander's eyes so he will love his former sweetheart, Hermia. He leaves Demetrius loving Helena.
9. Finding the two couples asleep in the wood and learning of their more balanced love, what order does Theseus give?
    He orders that they should follow him and Hippolyta to be married with them at the temple.
10. Why do you think Shakespeare included a play within a play?
    The story of Pyramus and Thisby is an ancient tale well known to the audiences in Shakespeare's time. The audience of *A Midsummer Night's Dream* could join in with the jests and comments.
11. What is the purpose of Puck's last speech?
    It closes the play and thanks the audience, asking that they enjoy or else pardon a frivolous entertainment.

III. Composition Answers will vary.

IV. Vocabulary
    Choose ten vocabulary words and read them orally to your class so students can write them down.

ADVANCED SHORT ANSWER UNIT TEST - *A Midsummer Night's Dream*

I. Matching

___ 1. Egeus   A. Duke of Athens

___ 2. Lysander   B. Wants to play all the roles

___ 3. Theseus   C. Queen of the Fairies

___ 4. Hippolyta   D. Father of Hermia

___ 5. Oberon   E. Wrote "Pyramus and Thisby"

___ 6. Helena   F. Helena loves him, but he's to marry Hermia

___ 7. Puck   G. Hermia loves him

___ 8. Hermia   H. Plays Wall

___ 9. Titania   I. Robin Goodfellow

___ 10. Quince   J. Plays Lion

___ 11. Flute   K. Queen of the Amazons

___ 12. Demetrius   L. Plays Thisby

___ 13. Bottom   M. Tells Hermia's plans to Demetrius

___ 14. Snout   N. King of the Fairies

___ 15. Snug   O. Arranges to meet Lysander in the woods

A Midsummer Night's Dream Advanced Short Answer Unit Test Page 2

II. Short Answer

1. Explain why Puck is one of Shakespeare's most memorable characters.

2. Define "tragedy," "comedy," and "romance" in the literary sense of the words. Explain into what category or categories *A Midsummer Night's Dream* falls and why.

3. Compare and contrast the female characters in the play: Hermia, Helena, Titania, and Hippolyta.

4. Compare and contrast the male characters in the play: Lysander, Demetrius, Oberon and Theseus.

A Midsummer Night's Dream Advanced Short Answer Unit Test Page 3

5. What parallels are there between "Pyramus and Thisby" and *A Midsummer Night's Dream*?

6. How does *A Midsummer Night's Dream* portray people in love? Explain your answer using examples from the text.

Identify and explain the following quotations:
7. "Rather your eyes must with his judgement look."

8. "The course of true love never did run smooth."

9. "Lord, what fools these mortals be!"

10. "Methought I was enamour'd of an ass."

A Midsummer Night's Dream Advanced Short Answer Unit Test Page 4

III. Composition

Explain how *A Midsummer Night's Dream* shows "love is blind" and love is unreasonable and unpredictable. Use specific examples from the text to support your statements.

A Midsummer Night's Dream Advanced Short Answer Unit Test Page 5

III. Vocabulary

    Write down the vocabulary words you are given. Go back later and use all of those vocabulary words in a composition relating to *A Midsummer Night's Dream*.

MULTIPLE CHOICE UNIT TEST 1 - *A Midsummer Night's Dream*

I. Matching/Identify

___ 1. Egeus   A. Helena loves him, but he's to marry Hermia

___ 2. Lysander   B. Queen of the Amazons

___ 3. Theseus   C. Queen of the Fairies

___ 4. Hippolyta   D. Hermia loves him

___ 5. Oberon   E. Wrote "Pyramus and Thisby"

___ 6. Helena   F. Duke of Athens

___ 7. Puck   G. Father of Hermia

___ 8. Hermia   H. Wants to play all the roles

___ 9. Titania   I. Plays Lion

___ 10. Quince   J. Robin Goodfellow

___ 11. Flute   K. Plays Wall

___ 12. Demetrius   L. Tells Hermia's plans to Demetrius

___ 13. Bottom   M. Plays Thisby

___ 14. Snout   N. Arranges to meet Lysander in the woods

___ 15. Snug   O. King of the Fairies

A Midsummer Night's Dream Multiple Choice Unit Test 1 Page 2

II. Multiple Choice

1. What will be Hermia's fate if she refuses to marry Demetrius?
    A. She will become a servant in her father's house.
    B. She will be banished to the wilderness.
    C. She will have to choose to die or live as a cloistered nun.
    D. She will be blinded and driven off to live as a beggar.

2. To what do Lysander and Hermia agree?
    A. They will meet on the next night in the woods and escape to Lysander's aunt's house to be married.
    B. She will do as her father asks, but poison Demetrius soon after the marriage. Then she will marry Lysander.
    C. They will stand together and defy her father.
    D. They will go to the temple, make offerings to the gods, and ask for their help.

3. What hope does Helena have by telling Demetrius of Lysander and Hermia's flight?
    A. She is jealous and wants to get Hermia in as much trouble as possible.
    B. She anticipates the sweet pain of following him to and from the appointed wood while he pursues Hermia.
    C. She expects a monetary reward from Egeus for stopping Hermia.
    D. She wants Lysander to marry her instead.

4. On what mission does Oberon send Puck?
    A. Oberon sends Puck to find the parents of the young boy so they can rescue him.
    B. Oberon sends Puck to destroy the wedding feast by causing a great storm.
    C. Oberon sends Puck to find a flower that has been struck by Cupid's arrow, so he may anoint the sleeping Titania, causing her to blindly fall in love with the first creature she sees upon awakening.
    D. Oberon sends Puck to beg the queen to hear his requests.

5. Upon overhearing Demetrius and Helena, what does Oberon command Puck to do?
    A. Oberon commands Puck to send a message to Helena's father and tell him of her plan.
    B. Oberon sends Puck to make them have dreams about what the other will look like in forty years, so they will not want to marry each other.
    C. He sends Puck to cause a terrible storm that will force them to abandon their plan and return home.
    D. He sends Puck to anoint the boy's eyes as he sleeps so that upon waking he will see the maid and love her.

A Midsummer Night's Dream Multiple Choice Unit Test 1 Page 3

6. Upon whose eyes does Puck apply the potion?
   A. He does Hermia's eyes.
   B. He does Demetrius' eyes.
   C. He does Lysander's eyes.
   D. He does Egeus' eyes.

7. What has Puck done to Bottom?
   A. He has given Bottom hooves and a tail.
   B. He has changed Bottom's voice to a croak.
   C. He has changed Bottom's head into that of an ass.
   D. He has given Bottom claws for hands.

8. What remedy corrects the crossed-loved couples?
   A. The aroma from the woods clears their senses.
   B. Puck drips the potion on Lysander's eyes so he will again love Hermia.
   C. Oberon confronts them, tells them what happened, and asks them to make their own choices.
   D. One of the craftsmen plays a love tune that secretly whispers the names of their true loves to each of them.

9. Why do you think Shakespeare. included a play within a play?
   A. Pyramus and Thisbee is an ancient tale well known to audience in Shakespeare's time. The audience would appreciate the jests and comments.
   B. He had been commissioned to write a play of a certain length, and his fell short. The play within a play was a filler to use up time.
   C. He uses it as a semi-veiled political speech.
   D. He used it in place of an intermission, to help refocus the audience's attention.

10. The last speech of the play has many purposes. Which of these is not one of them?
    A. It closes the play.
    B. It thanks the audience.
    C. It asks that the audience enjoy or else pardon a frivolous entertainment.
    D. It reminds the audience that the actors will gladly accept monetary donations after the play.

A Midsummer Night's Dream Multiple Choice Unit Test 1 Page 4

III. Composition
    What are the three story lines of the play, and what holds them together?

A Midsummer Night's Dream Multiple Choice Unit Test 1 Page 5

IV. Vocabulary

___ 1. Amorous   a. Remaining or staying temporarily

___ 2. Broached   b. A cloth used to wrap a body for burial

___ 3. Perjured   c. A strongly held opinion; a conviction

___ 4. Upbraid   d. Gladness and gaiety

___ 5. Perforce   e. To show contempt for

___ 6. Tarrying   f. Pleasing to the ear; melodious

___ 7. Chink   g. Regretting deeply; mourning; expressing sorrow

___ 8. Lamenting   h. A period of decline

___ 9. Brake   i. Friendly and agreeable; good-natured

___ 10. Dulcet   j. A thicket

___ 11. Bower   k. To reproach

___ 12. Amiable   l. Verbal expression in speech or writing

___ 13. Discourse   m. A high ridge of land or rock jutting out into a body of water

___ 14. Consecrated   n. Sacred

___ 15. Mirth   o. A narrow opening; a crack

___ 16. Flout   p. By necessity; by force of circumstances

___ 17. Promontory   q. A woman's private chamber in a medieval castle

___ 18. Wane   r. Strongly attracted or disposed to love

___ 19. Persuasion   s. Testified falsely under oath; falsified; untrue

___ 20. Shroud   t. Pierced in order to draw off liquid

MULTIPLE CHOICE UNIT TEST 2 - *A Midsummer Night's Dream*

I. Matching/Identify

___ 1. Egeus   A. Duke of Athens

___ 2. Lysander   B. Wants to play all the roles

___ 3. Theseus   C. Queen of the Fairies

___ 4. Hippolyta   D. Father of Hermia

___ 5. Oberon   E. Wrote "Pyramus and Thisby"

___ 6. Helena   F. Helena loves him, but he's to marry Hermia

___ 7. Puck   G. Hermia loves him

___ 8. Hermia   H. Plays Wall

___ 9. Titania   I. Robin Goodfellow

___ 10. Quince   J. Plays Lion

___ 11. Flute   K. Queen of the Amazons

___ 12. Demetrius   L. Plays Thisby

___ 13. Bottom   M. Tells Hermia's plans to Demetrius

___ 14. Snout   N. King of the Fairies

___ 15. Snug   O. Arranges to meet Lysander in the woods

A Midsummer Night's Dream Multiple Choice Unit Test 2 Page 2

II. Multiple Choice

1. What will be Hermia's fate if she refuses to marry Demetrius?
    A. She will have to choose to die or live as a cloistered nun.
    B. She will be banished to the wilderness.
    C. She will become a servant in her father's house.
    D. She will be blinded and driven off to live as a beggar.

2. To what do Lysander and Hermia agree?
    A. They will stand together and defy her father.
    B. She will do as her father asks, but poison Demetrius soon after the marriage. Then she will marry Lysander.
    C. They will meet on the next night in the woods and escape to Lysander's aunt's house to be married.
    D. They will go to the temple, make offerings to the gods, and ask for their help.

3. What hope does Helena have by telling Demetrius of Lysander and Hermia's flight?
    A. She is jealous and wants to get Hermia in as much trouble as possible.
    B. She wants Lysander to marry her instead.
    C. She expects a monetary reward from Egeus for stopping Hermia.
    D. She anticipates the sweet pain of following him to and from the appointed wood while he pursues Hermia.

4. On what mission does Oberon send Puck?
    A. Oberon sends Puck to find the parents of the young boy so they can rescue him.
    B. Oberon sends Puck to find a flower that has been struck by Cupid's arrow, so he may anoint the sleeping Titania, causing her to blindly fall in love with the first creature she sees upon awakening.
    C. Oberon sends Puck to destroy the wedding feast by causing a great storm.
    D. Oberon sends Puck to beg the queen to hear his requests.

5. Upon overhearing Demetrius and Helena, what does Oberon command Puck to do?
    A. He sends Puck to anoint the boy's eyes as he sleeps so that upon waking he will see the maid and love her.
    B. Oberon sends Puck to make them have dreams about what the other will look like in forty years, so they will not want to marry each other.
    C. He sends Puck to cause a terrible storm that will force them to abandon their plan and return home.
    D. Oberon commands Puck to send a message to Helena's father and tell him of her plan.

A Midsummer Night's Dream Multiple Choice Unit Test 1 Page 3

6. Upon whose eyes does Puck apply the potion?
    A. He does Lysander's eyes.
    B. He does Demetrius' eyes.
    C. He does Hermia's eyes.
    D. He does Egeus' eyes.

7. What has Puck done to Bottom?
    A. He has given Bottom hooves and a tail.
    B. He has changed Bottom's voice to a croak.
    C. He has given Bottom claws for hands.
    D. He has changed Bottom's head into that of an ass.

8. What remedy corrects the crossed-loved couples?
    A. The aroma from the woods clears their senses.
    B. Oberon confronts them, tells them what happened, and asks them to make their own choices.
    C. Puck drips the potion on Lysander's eyes so he will again love Hermia.
    D. One of the craftsmen plays a love tune that secretly whispers the names of their true loves to each of them.

9. Why do you think Shakespeare included a play within a play?
    A. He used it in place of an intermission, to help refocus the audience's attention.
    B. He had been commissioned to write a play of a certain length, and his fell short. The play within a play was a filler to use up time.
    C. He uses it as a semi-veiled political speech.
    D. Pyramus and Thisby is an ancient tale well known to audience in Shakespeare's time. The audience would appreciate the jests and comments.

10. The last speech of the play has many purposes. Which of these is not one of them?
    A. It reminds the audience that the actors will gladly accept monetary donations after the play.
    B. It thanks the audience.
    C. It asks that the audience enjoy or else pardon a frivolous entertainment.
    D. It closes the play.

III. Composition
1. Compare and contrast the female characters in the play: Hermia, Helena, Titania, and Hippolyta.

2. Compare and contrast the male characters in the play: Lysander, Demetrius, Oberon, and Theseus.

A Midsummer Night's Dream Multiple Choice Unit Test 2 Page 5

IV. Vocabulary

___ 1. Kindred
___ 2. Conjunction
___ 3. Enamored
___ 4. Shroud
___ 5. Undistinguishable
___ 6. Fret
___ 7. Loath
___ 8. Discretion
___ 9. Broached
___ 10. Rheumatic
___ 11. Rebuke
___ 12. Base
___ 13. Spurn
___ 14. Discourse
___ 15. Abjure
___ 16. Audacious
___ 17. Dulcet
___ 18. Chink
___ 19. Extempore
___ 20. Valor

a. Ability or power to decide responsibly
b. To give up; abstain from
c. Pierced in order to draw off liquid
d. The lowest or bottom part
e. Spoken or carried out with little preparation
f. Verbal expression in speech or writing
g. Of, relating to, or suffering from aches in the muscles, joints or bones
h. To criticize or reprove sharply; reprimand
i. Worry
j. A cloth used to wrap a body for burial
k. To kick at or tread on disdainfully
l. Pleasing to the ear; melodious
m. Be unwilling or reluctant; be disinclined
n. Bravery; courage
o. Inspired with love; captivated
p. A joint or simultaneous occurrence
q. Bold, insolent, spirited or original
r. Having no unique markings; can't be clearly seen
s. A narrow opening; a crack
t. Relatives

ANSWER SHEET - *A Midsummer Night's Dream*
Multiple Choice Unit Tests

I. Matching
1. ___
2. ___
3. ___
4. ___
5. ___
6. ___
7. ___
8. ___
9. ___
10. ___
11. ___
12. ___
13. ___
14. ___
15. ___

II. Multiple Choice
1. ___
2. ___
3. ___
4. ___
5. ___
6. ___
7. ___
8. ___
9. ___
10. ___

IV. Vocabulary
1. ___
2. ___
3. ___
4. ___
5. ___
6. ___
7. ___
8. ___
9. ___
10. ___
11. ___
12. ___
13. ___
14. ___
15. ___
16. ___
17. ___
18. ___
19. ___
20. ___

ANSWER KEY - *A Midsummer Night's Dream*
Multiple Choice Unit Tests

Answers to Unit Test 1 are in the left column. Answers to Unit Test 2 are in the right column.

I. Matching	II. Multiple Choice	IV. Vocabulary
1. G D	1. C A	1. R T
2. D G	2. A C	2. T P
3. F A	3. B D	3. S O
4. B K	4. C B	4. K J
5. O N	5. D A	5. P R
6. L M	6. C A	6. A I
7. J I	7. C D	7. O M
8. N O	8. B C	8. G A
9. C C	9. A D	9. J C
10. E E	10. D A	10. F G
11. M L		11. Q H
12. A F		12. I D
13. H B		13. L K
14. K H		14. N F
15. I J		15. D B
		16. E Q
		17. M L
		18. H S
		19. C E
		20. B N

UNIT RESOURCE MATERIALS

BULLETIN BOARD IDEAS - *A Midsummer Night's Dream*

1. Save one corner of the board for the best of students' *A Midsummer Night's Dream* writing assignments.

2. Take one of the word search puzzles from the extra activities section and with a marker copy it over in a large size on the bulletin board. Write the clue words to find to one side. Invite students prior to and after class to find the words and circle them on the bulletin board.

3. Write several of the most significant quotations from the book onto the board on brightly colored paper.

4. Make a bulletin board listing the vocabulary words for this unit. As you complete sections of the novel and discuss the vocabulary for each section, write the definitions on the bulletin board. (If your board is one students face frequently, it will help them learn the words.)

5. Make a bulletin board about courtship and marriage. Post articles and pictures from our own culture, Shakespeare's times, or about various cultures from around the world.

6. Post articles of criticism about the play.

7. Do a bulletin board about Shakespeare. Post a brief summary of his life next to his picture. All around the bulletin board, post "playbills" for each of his major works with a little summary of the plot of each play written inside.

8. As an alternate introductory activity, prepare a bulletin board with the title SHAKESPEARE on background paper with his picture in the middle of the board. Ask each student to write one fact, the title of a play, a quote, or anything he/she knows relating to Shakespeare.

9. Make a humorous bulletin board about love and marriage. Post pictures of the romantic side of love and marriage on one side (You know the type--couples running towards each other in fields of flowers, sailing on yachts together into the sunset, walking on beautiful beaches without another person in sight....) and the responsibilities and realities of love and marriage on the other (Getting up with ugly curlers in your hair in the morning, wiping up spills from the kid in the high chair, scrubbing the tile in the bathroom, sitting down with the checkbook and a stack of bills ....).

EXTRA ACTIVITIES - *Midsummer Night's Dream*

One of the difficulties in teaching a novel is that all students don't read at the same speed. One student who likes to read may take the book home and finish it in a day or two. Sometimes a few students finish the in-class assignments early. The problem, then, is finding suitable extra activities for students.

One thing you can do is to keep a little library in the classroom. For this unit on *A Midsummer Night's Dream*, you might check out from the school library other plays by Shakespeare. A biography or articles about the author would be interesting for some students. You can include other books and articles about courtship and marriage, dreams and dreaming, fairies, history of the period, humor, jokes and riddles, careers in the theater, or articles about Shakespearian/Elizabethan theater, or articles of criticism about *A Midsummer Night's Dream*.

Other things you may keep on hand are puzzles. We have made some relating directly to *A Midsummer Night's Dream* for you. Feel free to duplicate them.

Some students may like to draw. You might devise a contest or allow some extra-credit grade for students who draw characters or scenes from *A Midsummer Night's Dream*. Note, too, that if the students do not want to keep their drawings you may pick up some extra bulletin board materials this way. If you have a contest and you supply the prize (a CD or something like that perhaps), you could, possibly, make the drawing itself a non-refundable entry fee.

The pages which follow contain games, puzzles and worksheets. The keys, when appropriate, immediately follow the puzzle or worksheet. There are two main groups of activities: one group for the unit; that is, generally relating to the *Midsummer Night's Dream* text, and another group of activities related strictly to the *Midsummer Night's Dream* vocabulary.

Directions for these games, puzzles and worksheets are self-explanatory. The object here is to provide you with extra materials you may use in any way you choose.

MORE ACTIVITIES - *A Midsummer Night's Dream*

1. Have students design a playbill for *A Midsummer Night's Dream*.

2. Have students design a bulletin board (ready to be put up) for *A Midsummer Night's Dream.*

3. Use some of the related topics (noted earlier for an in-class library) as topics for research, reports or written papers, or as topics for guest speakers.

4. Invite a marriage counselor in to talk to students about courtship and marriage in our society today.

5. Research courtship in the 1600s and/or the history of courtship through the ages.

6. Instead of making a whole production, assign a character to each student. Have students design their own costumes, memorize a short passage from the play, and recite the passage (in costume) in front of the class.

7. Compare and contrast *A Midsummer Night's Dream* with a modern comedy about love.

8. After analyzing Shakespeare's poetry, have students experiment imitating his style by rewriting the end of the play.

9. Have students research careers in the theater, acting, and movies as well as careers related to courtship and marriage (preacher, dating service, tuxedo rental business, catering, floral shop, etc.).

10. Have students plan and carry out a mock wedding, making all the necessary arrangements including (but not limited to) invitations, flowers, cake, reception, service, attire, decorations, schedule of events, and music. Make sure they find the real costs of items they need.

11. Spend a class period talking about fairies in literature through the years.

WORD SEARCH - *A Midsummer Night's Dream*

All words in this list are associated with *A Midsummer Night's Dream*. The words are placed backwards, forward, diagonally, up and down. The included words are listed below the word searches.

```
Y L L Q L R J K Z J L V P V J H Q G M H F Z T M
Y M O N S H O Z T M X F R G S G M U E V Q U N L
L G K V F B R P A N L W T Z Y J W L I T O J Z D
P U C K E R A E P S E K A H S U E G E N U N H J
M R W R W G R L D D B M S L E N F G S B C L K D
F W O G F D X K D N C O E K A S Z L A R J E F J
W N V L T E Z I W P A Y T G A I E R O T F S R Y
E U G N O T N L L A W S C T D T M U D W S E Y E
G Q K K L G N E I N T T Y P O U T R S A E N K S
S C X J P L U N C V N L B L M M J J E V B R U C
H J G Y Y F A E G S O N V X M N J C X H C R B G
Z Y X M D T S L H P S C T D E M E T R I U S T M
J T N N I D Z L P T D C Z H J H V M B W D M S P
C V K T O P F I C Z A L L Q G Y W T R N M B Y V
W W M O S B H C P K G C S C P Z K G H R T T P W
S P W V N W M F L T M G C B R W F L N S P B L Y
M I D S U M M E R M F W L F P J J X H G C S Y D
```

ACT	FLUTE	NUN	SNUG
ASS	HELENA	OBERON	STAGE
BOTTOM	HERMIA	PROLOGUE	THESEUS
DEMETRIUS	HIPPOLYTA	PUCK	TITANIA
DREAM	JUDGEMENT	QUINCE	TONGUE
EGEUS	LOVE	SCENE	WALL
EYES	LYSANDER	SHAKESPEARE	WEDDING
FLOWER	MIDSUMMER	SNOUT	WOODS

KEY: WORD SEARCH - *A Midsummer Night's Dream*

All words in this list are associated with *A Midsummer Night's Dream*. The words are placed backwards, forward, diagonally, up and down. The included words are listed below the word searches.

```
            L                                   Q     H       T
              O       O    T M                    U E       U
                V  B R    A N   W T                 L I T O
         P U C K E R A E P S E K A H S U E G E N U N
            R    R      R    D D B M       E N F G S    C L
              O      D      D N   O E    A S    L A       E F
            N    L    E    I      A    T G A I E    O T    S
         E U G N O T N L L A W S    T D    M U    W S E Y E
                    G    E I         Y    O U    R S A E N
                      U N C      L    L    M J    E       R U
                        A E    S O                 H          G
                        T S       P    T D E M E T R I U S
                      I D       P       C
                    T O       I       A
                   O      H
                 W
               M I D S U M M E R
```

ACT	FLUTE	NUN	SNUG
ASS	HELENA	OBERON	STAGE
BOTTOM	HERMIA	PROLOGUE	THESEUS
DEMETRIUS	HIPPOLYTA	PUCK	TITANIA
DREAM	JUDGEMENT	QUINCE	TONGUE
EGEUS	LOVE	SCENE	WALL
EYES	LYSANDER	SHAKESPEARE	WEDDING
FLOWER	MIDSUMMER	SNOUT	WOODS

CROSSWORD - *A Midsummer Night's Dream*

CROSSWORD CLUES - A Midsummer Night's Dream

ACROSS
2. Play division
6. Father of Hermia
8. Tells Hermia's plans to Demetrius
11. Robin Goodfellow
12. Looked with his eyes
13. Negative answer
14. Act division
15. Topic Theseus and Hippolyta discuss at play's start
17. Not real
18. Where Lysander & Hermia agree to meet
22. Queen of the Amazons
25. A single
28. Wants to play all the roles
29. Plays Wall
31. Coordinating conjunction
34. Revise
35. 'Tie up my love's ----, bring him silently'
36. Shakespeare
38. 'Your eyes must look with his ---'
40. Author
42. Helena ----s the actions of Lysander to being a cruel joke; relates to a particular cause or source

DOWN
1. Helena loves him, but he is to marry Hermia
2. Puck changes Bottom's head to that of an ---
3. Duke of Athens
4. Oberon sends Puck to find one struck by Cupid's arrow
5. Plays Thisby
7. Oberon commands Puck to anoint Demetrisus's Demetrius's --- as he sleeps
9. Hermia will have to live as one if she refuses to marry Demetrius
10. Writes 'Pyramus and Thisby'
16. A Midsummer Night's ---
18. What P & T talked through
19. King of the Fairies
20. Opposite of hate
21. Hermia loves him
22. Arranges to meet Lysander in the woods
23. Bottom wants one written for the play
24. Where plays are performed
26. A --- Night's Dream
27. Oberon ----s Puck to go look for a flower...; gives a direction or order
30. Queen of the Fairies
32. Plays Lion
33. Puck expressed --- to the audience; gratitude
37. Slang for getting married 'tie the ---'
39. Watch someone without their knowing it
41. Pronoun for Lysander

CROSSWORD ANSWER KEY - *A Midsummer Night's Dream*

```
D . . . A C T . F . . . . . F . . . . .
E G E U S . H E L E N A . . L . . . . Q
M . Y . S . E . O . U . . P U C K . . U
E . E . . . S A W . N O . . T . . . . I
T . S C E N E . E . . . . W E D D I N G
R . . . . U N R E A L . . . . R . . . C
I . W O O D S . . . . . L . L . . . . E
U . A . B . . . H I P P O L Y T A . . .
S . L . E . . . E . . . R . S . M . . .
. . L . R . S . R . O N E . A . . . . M
. I . B O T T O M . L . . . S N O U T I
A N D . N . A . I . O . . . D . . I . D
. S S . . . G . A . G . T . E D I T . S
. T O N G U E . . A U T H O R . . A . U
. . R . U . . . K . E . A . . . . N . M
. J U D G E M E N T . . N . S . I . . M
. . C . . . . . O . S H A K E S P E A R E
A T T R I B U T E . . . E . S . . Y . R
```

116

MATCHING QUIZ/WORKSHEET 1 - *A Midsummer Night's Dream*

___ 1. PROLOGUE   A. Bottom wants one written for the play

___ 2. DREAM   B. Hermia loves him

___ 3. WALL   C. Author

___ 4. QUINCE   D. What P & T talked through

___ 5. DEMETRIUS   E. Oberon commands Puck to anoint Demetrius's --- as he sleeps

___ 6. THESEUS   F. Write 'Pyramus and Thisby'

___ 7. HERMIA   G. Father of Hermia

___ 8. NUN   H. Duke of Athens

___ 9. SCENE   I. Helena loves, but he is to marry Hermia

___ 10. TONGUE   J. Puck changes Bottom's head to that of an ---

___ 11. EGEUS   K. Queen of the Amazons

___ 12. JUDGEMENT   L. Hermia will have to live as one if she refuses to marry Demetrius

___ 13. HIPPOLYTA   M. Plays Wall

___ 14. PUCK   N. Arranges to meet Lysander in the woods

___ 15. SNOUT   O. Act division

___ 16. EYES   P. 'Your eyes must look with his ---'

___ 17. FLOWER   Q. 'Tie up my love's ----, bring him silently'

___ 18. ASS   R. Robin Goodfellow

___ 19. SHAKESPEARE   S. Oberon sends Puck to find one struck by Cupid's arrow

___ 20. LYSANDER   T. A Midsummer Night's ---

KEY: MATCHING QUIZ/WORKSHEET 1 - *A Midsummer Night's Dream*

_A_ 1. PROLOGUE   A. Bottom wants one written for the play

_T_ 2. DREAM   B. Hermia loves him

_D_ 3. WALL   C. Author

_F_ 4. QUINCE   D. What P & T talked through

_I_ 5. DEMETRIUS   E. Oberon commands Puck to anoint Demetrius's --- as he sleeps

_H_ 6. THESEUS   F. Write 'Pyramus and Thisby'

_N_ 7. HERMIA   G. Father of Hermia

_L_ 8. NUN   H. Duke of Athens

_O_ 9. SCENE   I. Helena loves, but he is to marry Hermia

_Q_ 10. TONGUE   J. Puck changes Bottom's head to that of an ---

_G_ 11. EGEUS   K. Queen of the Amazons

_P_ 12. JUDGEMENT   L. Hermia will have to live as one if she refuses to marry Demetrius

_K_ 13. HIPPOLYTA   M. Plays Wall

_R_ 14. PUCK   N. Arranges to meet Lysander in the woods

_M_ 15. SNOUT   O. Act division

_E_ 16. EYES   P. 'Your eyes must look with his ---'

_S_ 17. FLOWER   Q. 'Tie up my love's ----, bring him silently'

_J_ 18. ASS   R. Robin Goodfellow

_C_ 19. SHAKESPEARE   S. Oberon sends Puck to find one struck by Cupid's arrow

_B_ 20. LYSANDER   T. A Midsummer Night's ---

MATCHING QUIZ/WORKSHEET 2 - *A Midsummer Night's Dream*

___ 1. EYES A. Puck changes Bottom's head to that of an ---

___ 2. MIDSUMMER B. Queen of the Fairies

___ 3. JUDGEMENT C. A --- Night's Dream

___ 4. STAGE D. Opposite of hate

___ 5. WEDDING E. Hermia loves him

___ 6. FLUTE F. Duke of Athens

___ 7. WOODS G. Where Lysander & Hermia agree to meet

___ 8. HIPPOLYTA H. Plays Thisby

___ 9. NUN I. 'Tie up my love's ----, bring him silently'

___ 10. HERMIA J. Author

___ 11. LYSANDER K. Oberon commands Puck to anoint Demetrius's --- as he sleeps

___ 12. ASS L. Hermia will have to live as one if she refuses to marry Demetrius

___ 13. TITANIA M. A Midsummer Night's ---

___ 14. LOVE N. 'Your eyes must look with his ---'

___ 15. TONGUE O. Topic Theseus and Hippolyta discuss at play's start

___ 16. DREAM P. Robin Goodfellow

___ 17. SHAKESPEARE Q. Arranges to meet Lysander in the woods

___ 18. SCENE R. Act division

___ 19. PUCK S. Where plays are performed

___ 20. THESEUS T. Queen of the Amazons

KEY: MATCHING QUIZ/WORKSHEET 2 - *A Midsummer Night's Dream*

K   1. EYES   A. Puck changes Bottom's head to that of an ---
C   2. MIDSUMMER   B. Queen of the Fairies
N   3. JUDGEMENT   C. A --- Night's Dream
S   4. STAGE   D. Opposite of hate
O   5. WEDDING   E. Hermia loves him
H   6. FLUTE   F. Duke of Athens
G   7. WOODS   G. Where Lysander & Hermia agree to meet
T   8. HIPPOLYTA   H. Plays Thisby
L   9. NUN   I. 'Tie up my love's ----, bring him silently'
Q   10. HERMIA   J. Author
E   11. LYSANDER   K. Oberon commands Puck to anoint Demetrius's --- as he sleeps
A   12. ASS   L. Hermia will have to live as one if she refuses to marry Demetrius
B   13. TITANIA   M. A Midsummer Night's ---
D   14. LOVE   N. 'Your eyes must look with his ---'
I   15. TONGUE   O. Topic Theseus and Hippolyta discuss at play's start
M   16. DREAM   P. Robin Goodfellow
J   17. SHAKESPEARE   Q. Arranges to meet Lysander in the woods
R   18. SCENE   R. Act division
P   19. PUCK   S. Where plays are performed
F   20. THESEUS   T. Queen of the Amazons

JUGGLE LETTER REVIEW GAME CLUE SHEET - *A Midsummer Night's Dream*

SCRAMBLED	WORD	CLUE
YPIATPOHL	HIPPOLYTA	Queen of the Amazons
ESEY	EYES	Oberon commands Puck to anoint Demetrius's --- as he sleeps
NNU	NUN	Hermia will have to live as one if she refuses to marry Demetrius
NEOOBR	OBERON	King of the Fairies
ADYLESRN	LYSANDER	Hermia loves him
UDSIREMET	DEMETRIUS	Helena loves, but he is to marry Hermia
CTA	ACT	Play division
CPKU	PUCK	Robin Goodfellow
UFTEL	FLUTE	Plays Thisby
ENCSE	SCENE	Act division
EHAELN	HELENA	Tells Hermia's plans to Demetrius
GPEOLURO	PROLOGUE	Bottom wants one written for the play
MAIHRE	HERMIA	Arranges to meet Lysander in the woods
DIWDGEN	WEDDING	Topic Theseus and Hippolyta discuss at play's start
UENIQC	QUINCE	Write 'Pyramus and Thisby'
EUTONG	TONGUE	'Tie up my love's ---, bring him silently'
SEUEG	EGEUS	Father of Hermia
UTSON	SNOUT	Plays Wall
UNTMGDJEE	JUDGEMENT	'Your eyes must look with his ----'
ATTIANI	TITANIA	Queen of the Fairies
EADMR	DREAM	A Midsummer Night's ---
SAS	ASS	Puck changes Bottom's head to that of an ---
GSTEA	STAGE	Where plays are performed
LLWA	WALL	What P & T talked through
GUSN	SNUG	Plays Lion
SSEUTHE	THESEUS	Duke of Athens
RAKAEESSPHE	SHAKESPEARE	Author
OTBMTO	BOTTOM	Wants to play all the roles
SDOOW	WOODS	Where Lysander & Hermia agree to meet

VOCABULARY RESOURCE MATERIALS

VOCABULARY WORD SEARCH - *A Midsummer Night's Dream*

All words in this list are associated with *A Midsummer Night's Dream* with an emphasis on the vocabulary words chosen for study in the text. The words are placed backwards, forward, diagonally, up and down. The included words are listed below.

```
D Z G G B T Y H B N C Q P Y B Y G B R B Z B F W
H T J M E R F A J M H R J R M M Y O F C O P P E
D P K C D S S R I T H F A N W R L R N W H S T Q
F I L C H E D R E B U K E L O A T H E N M I T Y
E U S R P U T L E T E S I T V I N R N C R Q N R
D N W C O H B A N V R N N N A D S E F P O U R K
V B A R R A D E R U E O T B D R O A S L Y U P D
J I H M I E C E O C M N J W E R H T U Z O U N S
K S S M O R T C H O E U U S I G E E A S R U Z T
G N A A O R S I R C R S U E G S U D U G R T T D
G N A F G I E P O E A O N N U P T I E M E E E J
F Z R V D E N D J N I O I O B V C Q L L A R P T
B E H G E L K R Q C B Y R R C J G P P E U T R T
P V T J P R T T A H R O A B L K D A F J D Y I C
C B M D S X Y D T R M I L B K R H H R K G X K C
G S K Z Y H U S A A D J S Z D C X E H K S W K R
H B R Q N A V T N N J S M E R O P M E T X E L J
```

ABJURE	CONSECRATED	FRET	RECOUNT
AMIABLE	DISCOURSE	KINDRED	REVENUE
AMOROUS	DISCRETION	KNAVERY	RHEUMATIC
AUDACIOUS	DOTAGE	LOATH	SHROUD
BASE	DULCET	MIRTH	SPRITE
BEGUILED	ENAMORED	PERFORCE	SPURN
BOWER	ENMITY	PERJURED	TARRYING
BRAKE	ENTWIST	PERSUASION	UPBRAID
BROACHED	EXTEMPORE	PROMONTORY	VALOR
CHAPLET	FILCHED	PURGE	VISAGE
CHINK	FLOUT	REBUKE	WANE

KEY: VOCABULARY WORD SEARCH - *A Midsummer Night's Dream*

All words in this list are associated with *A Midsummer Night's Dream* with an emphasis on the vocabulary words chosen for study in the text. The words are placed backwards, forward, diagonally, up and down. The included words are listed below.

```
                    T       B               B       R       B
                E   F A   M           R       Y O   C O         E
        D   C D   S R I         A N W R L R     W H     T
        F I L C H E D R E B U K E L O A T H E N M I T Y
        E U S     U T L E T E S I T V I N R     C R     N
        D N   C O H B A   V R N N N A D S E F P O U     K
        V   A R R A D E R U E O T B D R O A S L   U P
          I H M I E C E O C M N J W E R H T U     O U N S
        K S S M O R T C H O E U U S I G E E A S R U     T
          N A A O R S I R C R S U E G S U D U G R T T D
            A F G I E P O E A O N N U P T I E M E E E
            R V D E   D   N I O I O B         L L A R P
          E   E             C   Y R R C         P E U T
        P         R     A   R O A B       A     J D     I
                  Y D   R M I             H     R           C
                  U   A A D                 C   E
                A   T             E R O P M E T X E
```

ABJURE	CONSECRATED	FRET	RECOUNT
AMIABLE	DISCOURSE	KINDRED	REVENUE
AMOROUS	DISCRETION	KNAVERY	RHEUMATIC
AUDACIOUS	DOTAGE	LOATH	SHROUD
BASE	DULCET	MIRTH	SPRITE
BEGUILED	ENAMORED	PERFORCE	SPURN
BOWER	ENMITY	PERJURED	TARRYING
BRAKE	ENTWIST	PERSUASION	UPBRAID
BROACHED	EXTEMPORE	PROMONTORY	VALOR
CHAPLET	FILCHED	PURGE	VISAGE
CHINK	FLOUT	REBUKE	WANE

VOCABULARY CROSSWORD - *A Midsummer Night's Dream*

VOCABULARY CROSSWORD CLUES - *A Midsummer Night's Dream*

ACROSS

4. Verbal expression in speech or writing
8. The lowest or bottom part
9. A cloth used to wrap a body for burial
10. A woman's private chamber in a medieval castle
12. A narrow opening; a crack
13. Unprincipled; crafty
15. A wreath or garland for the head
16. Make a mistake
18. Opposite of under
20. Opposite of hate
22. Strongly attracted or disposed to love
23. It and tide stop for no man
24. A prearranged outing by a courting couple
26. To remove (impurities) by or as if by cleansing
27. To give up; abstain from
29. A deterioration of mental faculties; senility
31. Oberon commands Puck to anoint Demetrius's --- as he sleeps
34. Play division
35. Snitched; stole
37. To narrate the facts or details of
39. Hermia will have to live as one if she refuses to marry Demetrius
41. Kind of reading done aloud
42. A ghost or soul
43. Gladness and gaiety
44. Plays Wall
45. Tells Hermia's plans to Demetrius
47. Unusual
48. Plays Thisby
49. Ability or power to decide responsibly

DOWN

1. Puck changes Bottom's head to that of an ---
2. Worry
3. Bold, insolent, spirited or original
5. Sacred
6. To criticize or reprove sharply; reprimand
7. Inspired with love; captivated
8. A thicket
9. To kick at or tread on disdainfully
10. Deluded; cheated; diverted
11. A period of decline
12. Noisy
14. Bravery; courage
17. Pleasing to the ear; melodious
19. Deep-seated, often mutual hatred
21. Father of Hermia
22. Friendly and agreeable; good-natured
25. A joint or simultaneous occurrence
28. To reproach
30. Twist together
32. Spoken or carried out with little preparation
33. Relatives
35. To show contempt for
36. Be unwilling or reluctant; be disinclined
38. Slang for being unfaithful
40. Oberon sends Puck to find one struck by Cupid's arrow
42. Appears to be
44. Plays Lion
46. The final curtain; the last words of the last act

VOCABULARY CROSSWORD ANSWER KEY - *A Midsummer Night's Dream*

VOCABULARY WORKSHEET 1 - *A Midsummer Night's Dream*

___ 1. KINDRED	A. Ability or power to decide responsibly

___ 2. CONJUNCTION	B. To give up; abstain from

___ 3. ENAMORED	C. Pierced in order to draw off liquid

___ 4. SHROUD	D. The lowest or bottom part

___ 5. UNDISTINGUISHABLE	E. Spoken or carried out with little preparation

___ 6. FRET	F. Verbal expression in speech or writing

___ 7. LOATH	G. Of, relating to, or suffering from aches in the muscles, joints or bones

___ 8. DISCRETION	H. To criticize or reprove sharply; reprimand

___ 9. BROACHED	I. Worry

___ 10. RHEUMATIC	J. A cloth used to wrap a body for burial

___ 11. REBUKE	K. To kick at or tread on disdainfully

___ 12. BASE	L. Pleasing to the ear; melodious

___ 13. SPURN	M. Be unwilling or reluctant; be disinclined

___ 14. DISCOURSE	N. Bravery; courage

___ 15. ABJURE	O. Inspired with love; captivated

___ 16. AUDACIOUS	P. A joint or simultaneous occurrence

___ 17. DULCET	Q. Bold, insolent, spirited or original

___ 18. CHINK	R. Having no unique markings; can't be clearly seen

___ 19. EXTEMPORE	S. A narrow opening; a crack

___ 20. VALOR	T. Relatives

KEY: VOCABULARY WORKSHEET 1 - *A Midsummer Night's Dream*

T 1. KINDRED   A. Ability or power to decide responsibly

P 2. CONJUNCTION   B. To give up; abstain from

O 3. ENAMORED   C. Pierced in order to draw off liquid

J 4. SHROUD   D. The lowest or bottom part

R 5. UNDISTINGUISHABLE   E. Spoken or carried out with little preparation

I 6. FRET   F. Verbal expression in speech or writing

M 7. LOATH   G. Of, relating to, or suffering from aches in the muscles, joints or bones

A 8. DISCRETION   H. To criticize or reprove sharply; reprimand

C 9. BROACHED   I. Worry

G 10. RHEUMATIC   J. A cloth used to wrap a body for burial

H 11. REBUKE   K. To kick at or tread on disdainfully

D 12. BASE   L. Pleasing to the ear; melodious

K 13. SPURN   M. Be unwilling or reluctant; be disinclined

F 14. DISCOURSE   N. Bravery; courage

B 15. ABJURE   O. Inspired with love; captivated

Q 16. AUDACIOUS   P. A joint or simultaneous occurrence

L 17. DULCET   Q. Bold, insolent, spirited or original

S 18. CHINK   R. Having no unique markings; can't be clearly seen

E 19. EXTEMPORE   S. A narrow opening; a crack

N 20. VALOR   T. Relatives

VOCABULARY WORKSHEET 2 - *A Midsummer Night's Dream*

___ 1. A woman's private chamber in a medieval castle
    a. Bower   b. Knavery   c. Tarrying   d. Discourse

___ 2. To kick at or tread on disdainfully
    a. Spurn   b. Discourse   c. Rheumatic   d. Loath

___ 3. A high ridge of land or rock jutting out into a body of water
    a. Promontory   b. Chaplet   c. Mirth   d. Knavery

___ 4. Unprincipled; crafty
    a. Sprite   b. Knavery   c. Recount   d. Consecrated

___ 5. Testified falsely under oath; falsified; untrue
    a. Visage   b. Shroud   c. Brake   d. Perjured

___ 6. A deterioration of mental faculties; senility
    a. Recount   b. Dotage   c. Entwist   d. Amiable

___ 7. Snitched; stole
    a. Shroud   b. Enmity   c. Filched   d. Perforce

___ 8. Bold, insolent, spirited or original
    a. Chaplet   b. Extempore   c. Audacious   d. Bower

___ 9. A period of decline
    a. Broached   b. Chaplet   c. Chink   d. Wane

___ 10. Income; wealth
    a. Persuasion   b. Discourse   c. Rebuke   d. Revenue

___ 11. Bravery; courage
    a. Extempore   b. Amorous   c. Tarrying   d. Valor

___ 12. Ability or power to decide responsibly
    a. Kindred   b. Discretion   c. Loath   d. Lamenting

___ 13. Sacred
    a. Enmity   b. Loath   c. Audacious   d. Consecrated

___ 14. A thicket
    a. Brake   b. Promontory   c. Kindred   d. Discourse

___ 15. Twist together
    a. Bower   b. Enmity   c. Chink   d. Entwist

___ 16. To show contempt for
    a. Base   b. Amorous   c. Dulcet   d. Flout

___ 17. Spoken or carried out with little preparation
    a. Valor   b. Beguiled   c. Bower   d. Extempore

___ 18. Friendly and agreeable; good-natured
    a. Amiable   b. Discretion   c. Amorous   d. Flout

___ 19. By necessity; by force of circumstances
    a. Discourse   b. Visage   c. Perforce   d. Enmity

___ 20. Strongly attracted or disposed to love
    a. Flout   b. Spurn   c. Recount   d. Amorous

KEY: VOCABULARY WORKSHEET 2 - *A Midsummer Night's Dream*

__A__ 1. A woman's private chamber in a medieval castle
    a. Bower   b. Knavery   c. Tarrying   d. Discourse

__A__ 2. To kick at or tread on disdainfully
    a. Spurn   b. Discourse   c. Rheumatic   d. Loath

__A__ 3. A high ridge of land or rock jutting out into a body of water
    a. Promontory   b. Chaplet   c. Mirth   d. Knavery

__B__ 4. Unprincipled; crafty
    a. Sprite   b. Knavery   c. Recount   d. Consecrated

__D__ 5. Testified falsely under oath; falsified; untrue
    a. Visage   b. Shroud   c. Brake   d. Perjured

__B__ 6. A deterioration of mental faculties; senility
    a. Recount   b. Dotage   c. Entwist   d. Amiable

__C__ 7. Snitched; stole
    a. Shroud   b. Enmity   c. Filched   d. Perforce

__C__ 8. Bold, insolent, spirited or original
    a. Chaplet   b. Extempore   c. Audacious   d. Bower

__D__ 9. A period of decline
    a. Broached   b. Chaplet   c. Chink   d. Wane

__D__ 10. Income; wealth
    a. Persuasion   b. Discourse   c. Rebuke   d. Revenue

__D__ 11. Bravery; courage
    a. Extempore   b. Amorous   c. Tarrying   d. Valor

__B__ 12. Ability or power to decide responsibly
    a. Kindred   b. Discretion   c. Loath   d. Lamenting

__D__ 13. Sacred
    a. Enmity   b. Loath   c. Audacious   d. Consecrated

__A__ 14. A thicket
    a. Brake   b. Promontory   c. Kindred   d. Discourse

__D__ 15. Twist together
    a. Bower   b. Enmity   c. Chink   d. Entwist

__D__ 16. To show contempt for
    a. Base   b. Amorous   c. Dulcet   d. Flout

__D__ 17. Spoken or carried out with little preparation
    a. Valor   b. Beguiled   c. Bower   d. Extempore

__A__ 18. Friendly and agreeable; good-natured
    a. Amiable   b. Discretion   c. Amorous   d. Flout

__C__ 19. By necessity; by force of circumstances
    a. Discourse   b. Visage   c. Perforce   d. Enmity

__D__ 20. Strongly attracted or disposed to love
    a. Flout   b. Spurn   c. Recount   d. Amorous

VOCABULARY JUGGLE LETTER REVIEW GAME CLUES
A Midsummer Night's Dream

SCRAMBLED	WORD	CLUE
ERCRPFOE	PERFORCE	By necessity; by force of circumstances
PBADIRU	UPBRAID	To reproach
CTEDUL	DULCET	Pleasing to the ear; melodious
EURNEEV	REVENUE	Income; wealth
DSHROU	SHROUD	A cloth used to wrap a body for burial
ELIFDCH	FILCHED	Snitched; stole
EDULGEBI	BEGUILED	Deluded; cheated; diverted
NCUTNOJOCIN	CONJUNCTION	A joint or simultaneous occurrence
WRBOE	BOWER	A woman's private chamber in a medieval castle
HLEATCP	CHAPLET	A wreath or garland for the head
ETEXREMPO	EXTEMPORE	Spoken or carried out with little preparation
NOURTEC	RECOUNT	To narrate the facts or details of
EGAVSI	VISAGE	Face; appearance
KBUREE	REBUKE	To criticize or reprove sharply; reprimand
MEERNODA	ENAMORED	Inspired with love; captivated
EAALIMB	AMIABLE	Friendly and agreeable; good natured
EJRABY	ABJURE	To give up; abstain from
AWEN	WANE	A period of decline
SOUESICRD	DISCOURSE	Verbal expression in speech or writing
AGRNIYTR	TARRYING	Remaining or staying temporarily
DEUEPJRR	PERJURED	Testified falsely under oath; falsified; untrue
YTINME	ENMITY	Deep-seated often mutual hatred
RAUOSOM	AMOROUS	Strongly attracted or disposed to love
TRSEIP	SPRITE	A ghost or soul
BLEAANMLET	LAMENTABLE	Worthy of grief, mourning or regret
TPRROMNOYO	PROMONTORY	A high ridge of land or rock jutting out into a body of water
EOINDTISCR	DISCRETION	Ability or power to decide responsibly
ATOHL	LOATH	Be unwilling or reluctant; be disinclined
MRATIECHU	RHEUMATIC	Of, relating to, or suffering from aches in the muscles, joints or bones
RHTIM	MIRTH	Gladness and gaiety
EBAS	BASE	The lowest or bottom part
REKBA	BRAKE	A thicket
PNRSU	SPURN	To kick at or tread on disdainfully
IDEGBELU	BEGUILED	Deluded; cheated; diverted
AORVL	VALOR	Bravery; courage

CPSIA information can be obtained
at www.ICGtesting.com
Printed in the USA
LVHW050735270123
737935LV00006B/190